A Step-b

# SMA
# MEMORY

**Neerja Roy Chowdhury** has been teaching memory techniques for over a decade now, and has travelled nationally and internationally to train people in the art of remembering. She is a Guinness Book of World Records and Indochina Book of Records holder. She has also developed her own memory-training software. Presently, she is involved in developing a curriculum in memory techniques for several universities.

A Step-by-Step Guide to a

# SMARTER MEMORY

## Neerja Roy Chowdhury

RUPA

First published by
Rupa Publications India Pvt. Ltd 2015
7/16, Ansari Road, Daryaganj
New Delhi 110002

*Sales Centres:*
Allahabad Bengaluru Chennai
Hyderabad Jaipur Kathmandu
Kolkata Mumbai

Text copyright © Neerja Roy Chowdhury 2015
Illustration copyright © Bijan Samaddar 2015

While every effort has been made to verify the authenticity of the
information contained in this book, the publisher and the author are in
no way liable for the use of the information contained in this book.

ISBN: 978-81-291-3583-4

First impression 2015

10 9 8 7 6 5 4 3 2 1

The moral right of the author has been asserted.

Printed by Thomson Press India Ltd, Faridabad

*To my little daughter, Ivy*

# CONTENTS

# PREFACE

I have written this book to introduce basic memory techniques that can be used in academics as well as day-to-day life. The techniques provided in this book are unique and not taught in any school or college syllabus. They are useful and easy and you are never too young or old to learn them.

As a parent, if you want your children to speed up their memorization, this book is for you. This book is full of illustrations to make their learning fun and memorable. The techniques given in this book will make children concentrate and memorize faster. This book is in normal everyday English and is free of jargon.

This book has been written to provide students, professionals, teachers and parents with practical, logical, easy-to-follow processes for improving their memory.

This is an intensive memory training guide based on my many years of experience in the field of memory techniques. This book answers the need for a practical instruction on memory techniques and serves as a practice book for anyone who wants to improve his or her memory with a minimum of training.

This book can be used to provide memory training to beginners of all ages. It is also very useful for older students in need of memory techniques to get higher grades in competitive exams. It can also be used by professionals as a supplement to any other course.

Memory trainers who wish to use this book for their training programmes in schools, or in general, are free to do so. The book's step-by-step chapters are suitable for one-to-one teaching or regular classroom use.

To get most out of this book, I would recommend that you do the tests and exercises given in most of the chapters. These exercises are to ensure that your learning is on the right track.

If you have never used memory techniques before, you will be pleasantly surprised with the results.

# CHAPTER 1

-------------------------------------------------------------------

# THE SECRET MEMORY FORMULA

DEAR FOLKS, I welcome you to the fascinating world of memory. In the next few pages, I am going to share with you the **Secret Memory Formula**, which helped me to memorize the complete *Oxford English Hindi Dictionary* and helped me to become arguably the world's only person to memorize a dictionary. To make you understand the power of the Secret Memory Formula, let me share my story, I was born and brought up in a small town of Uttar Pradesh and studied throughout in Hindi Medium. It was only after my post-graduation, when I shifted to Delhi in search of a suitable career, that I understood the need and significance of learning the English language. At that time, English for me was almost as alien as Spanish or German, or for that matter any language of the world.

I tried all the conventionally available ways to learn English—from enrolling in coaching classes to learning through various self-learning tutorial books and audio CDs. It was only when I discovered the Secret Memory Formula that I was able to tap the infinite hidden potential of my brain, and within the next six months I could memorize the complete dictionary.

Now, in another few minutes, the Secret Memory Formula will be available to you and will help you to unlock that door in the brain which leads to faster memorising, permanent and long-term retention, and quick and correct recollection. Be it a long theory or a difficult formula, a complicated equation or a tongue-twisting scientific term or a definition, you will be on a superfast memory highway which you might not have experienced before.

As a student you know that you buy the best study material, go to renowned coaching classes, make a study schedule at home and try to effectively manage your time, sacrificing your play and socializing time. As the date for the assignment or exam approaches, you work even harder, do not sleep enough. You keep on revising and practising the important answers but when you take the exam you still fail to recollect the important points of a well-revised answer. You struggle hard and time runs out. When you come out of the examination hall you recall all the forgotten points, and it freaks you out. Your teachers say you are a sincere student, your parents admit you work hard, but your grades do not confirm it. It happens years after year. The same events and results almost every time indicate that you need to try a different way to succeed.

Memory failures do not spare you even after school and college life. As a professional you encounter so many events when poor memory embarrasses you. How many times are you unable to recall the exact content of your sales presentation, your close friend's birthday, your email password, ATM PIN or even your own anniversary? Quite often. You struggle on a day-to-day basis to recall the items you need to buy, the location where you parked your car and many more. Not only do such incidents create inconvenience, but they can be extremely annoying and frustrating, especially when there is no one to blame but yourself.

The Secret Memory Formula will not only help you comprehend why our brain behaves in such an unreliable manner, but will also help you create your own mental storage system so that your difficult and lengthy syllabus is easily locatable during the examination. You will be able to create your own dependable memory system which will help you to learn the syllabus faster, retain it for a longer period and recall it quickly and correctly.

This Secret Memory Formula will also save you from an embarrassing situation when you are not able to recollect the name of an old business associate, it will even help you memorize an unexpected business speech. This Secret Memory Formula will help you remember the sequence and the content of business negotiations and also various useful quotes.

As a welcome side-effect, you will realize that you are a person with better focus and concentration and your interest in the subject will dramatically increase.

Now let's begin the techniques with some experiments.

## Experiment 1

This experiment will help you to discover the Secret Memory Formula. Here you will need a friend.

**Step 1:** Find a friend who will read the matter in the box for you. Ask him to read it slowly.

You are wearing a **big cap** and brushing your teeth with **toothpaste**. There is a bucket full of water in front of you. While taking out water from the bucket, you drop your **mobile** in it. You think of fixing the mobile and open a **book**. As you open the book you see pictures of **red tomatoes** on each page of the book. You pick up one tomato and as you chop it, a car comes out of it. The **car** is loaded with **biscuits**. You drive the car but it runs out of petrol. You go to the **petrol station** but the attendant fills a **cold drink** in the car instead of petrol. Then the car is filled with cold drink, runs at a high speed and you are unable to control it. It rams into a bag of **sugar**. You scream for help and some people who are wearing **red jackets** come to your rescue. You find a beautiful **blue pen** in their pockets. You start drawing and painting with that pen on a **white bedsheet** in your house. A customer comes to buy the bed sheet and you try to tell the price with the help of a **calculator**. Suddenly, a white **dog** comes running, snatches the calculator and swallows it. As you chase the dog it falls into a drum filled with Asian **paint**. The dog is painted red when it comes out of the drum. Now the dog starts operating a **computer** and a **bike** comes out of the computer. The wheels of this bike are in the shape of **CDs**.

**Step 2:** While your friend is reading the matter in the box, close your eyes and while listening, try to visualize the entire chain of events in colour.

Now as you finished listening try the following test.

Fill in the blanks the words in the sequence in which you have heard.

1.  Big cap
2.  ............
3.  ............
4.  ............
5.  ............
6.  ............
7.  Car
8.  ............
9.  ............
10. Cold drink
11. ............
12. ............
13. Blue pen
14. ............
15. ............
16. ............
17. Asian paint
18. ............
19. ............
20. CDs

Now if you have visualized the corresponding images of all the words carefully, then you must have reproduced nearly all the words correctly.

## Experiment 2

Now prepare for the next experiment.

**Step 1:** Ask your friend to read the mobile number written in the box slowly.

9312286540

**Step 2:** Try to hear carefully with open/closed eyes, as you wish.

.

.

.

.

**Step 3:**

Try to recall the ten-digit number and write it here

--------------------------

**Conclusion:** With my experience of teaching memory techniques, I can tell you that the words in Experiment 1 are difficult for you to forget even in the long run, whereas the small ten-digit number would have been forgotten by now. Here, with the help of the above examples, I am going to help you discover the greatest science of human memory.

Take a moment and answer this—if we consider a video and an audio file of the same duration, which is the bigger and heavier file?

The video file, of course.

Now consider the following picture. Imagine that your brain is like a pot and most of the information that enters the brain (pot) is either through your eyes/imagination (video file) or through your ears (audio file).

Now suppose that pot (brain) has a leak and the size of the leak is bigger than the audio file, but smaller than the video file. This means information that will enter in the form of audio will never stay permanently, whereas whatever enters in the form of a video file will never be leaked and will stay permanently. And that is the mechanism of memory, the Secret Memory Formula, i.e. the video file is greater than the size of the memory leakage hole; and the memory leakage hole is greater than the audio file.

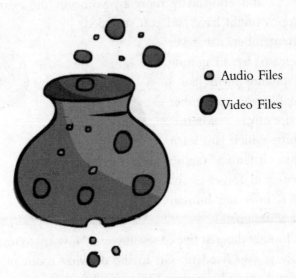

○ Audio Files

● Video Files

*Imagine your brain as a pot with infinite capacity but with a hole.*

**Video File >Memory Leakage Hole >Audio File**

## Now, answer the following questions:

1. The word just after bucket was (Experiment 1)
   _____

2. The word just before the bike was (Experiment 1)
   _____

3. The digit after the sixth-position number (Experiment 2) was _____

4. The digit just before number 8 (Experiment 2) was
   _____

I can bet that the first two questions must have been solved correctly and effortlessly more by you, but the next two questions might have had you stumped.

Remember, whatever you learn by imagining it in picture form like a video file you remember permanently, whereas anything which you learn by just listening (audio format) you forget easily. That is how the human brain is designed.

Think of the past five or seven years. Now, try to imagine the house you lived in. Go to the drawing room in your mind and try to locate the TV or identify the colour of the curtains, or even the design of the sofa set. I am sure you would have recalled it vividly.

But can you recollect the house number?

For most of us, the answer here will be 'no'.

That is the difference between the video and the audio file. The house number is the audio file and you will never be able to recollect it, if you don't get a chance to repeat it after some interval, while the inside/outside view of that old house is a video file you are not likely to  forget completely in your lifetime.

Now, you must have understood why you could never remember most of the content of your school syllabus permanently although you repeated it several times while you were in that class. Because the formulae, equations, scientific terms, long theories, geographical maps, various mathematics tables and other stuff, all come under the category of an audio file; and however hard you might have memorized it, eventually you are going to forget it.

Similarly in social situations you remember the faces but not the names, as the face is a video file and the name is an audio file.

Look at the Secret Memory Formula again:

**Video File >Memory Leakage Hole >Audio File**

It clearly suggests that whatever you want to learn permanently must be provided to the brain in a video file format.

But the question is how to convert our entire syllabus into a video file so as to learn it permanently. The answer lies in the brain's basic mechanism—**The Association Principle**.

----------------------------------------------------------------

# CHAPTER 2

# NEVER FORGET AN APPOINTMENT

W<small>HETHER</small> IT'S recalling an appointment, remembering a shopping list, or doing last minute preparation for the exams, the principle of memorising remains the same. For instance; if you are trying to learn swimming, will your academic background make any difference to your ability to learn swimming? Irrespective of whether you are a student of Science, Commerce, or Arts, the water in the swimming pool will remain the same and so will the principles of swimming. Similarly, regardless of what you intend to memorize—whether it is related to academics or remembering road maps—the principle of memorising remains exactly the same.

In the first chapter, we discussed one of the important principles of memory; the 'Law of Imagination', i.e. our brain is able to retain only that information which we are able to feed to in a video format as long-term memory.

One more important principle, which I introduced to you silently in the first chapter, is the 'Law of Association'. As you might have noticed, in the process of memorising the list of words while you were imagining the words, you were also associating them with one another. As a result, the sequence was held perfectly, and that's how you remembered it. But the same 'Law of Association' cannot be used with any information which is in audio format. For instance, a single digit or a number being an audio file kind of information without any pictures, cannot be associated and hence will not be remembered for long. That's why it becomes almost impossible to remember any information having digits or numbers—for example, remembering appointments, historical dates, or dates of birth, bank account numbers, complex passwords, etc.

This is where the role of memory techniques comes in. Primarily, the purpose of most memory techniques is to convert the information into a visual form and link it together in a manner or a sequence, in which you want to recall it. One such technique is called the **Shape Method**.

## The Shape Method

| | | |
|---|---|---|
| 0-Sun | | |

| | | |
|---|---|---|
| 5-Hook | 5 | |
| 6–Hockey Stick | 6 | |
| 7-Lamp-post | 7 | |
| 8-Spectacles | 8 | |

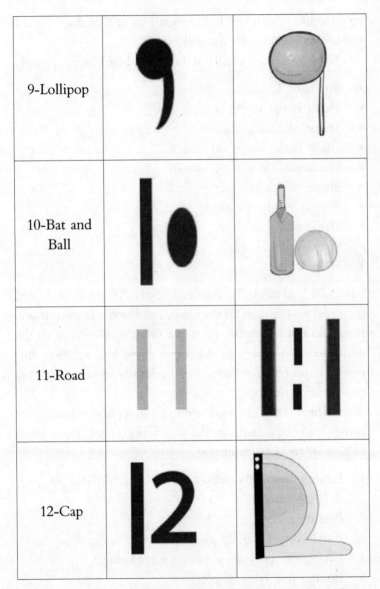

| 9-Lollipop | | |
| 10-Bat and Ball | | |
| 11-Road | | |
| 12-Cap | | |

Here, we simply connect each digit from 0 to 9 with a shape

or a picture which can help remind us of that digit. Take a minute to go through the following:

Now, let's take a small test. Fill in the blanks appropriately.

- Shape of 1.................
- Heart is the shape of...............
- Shape of 5.................
- Chair is the shape of...............
- Hockey Stick is the shape of...............
- Shape of 2.................
- Spectacles are the shape of...............
- Shape of 7...............
- Shape of 9...............
- Shape of 10.................

I am sure you might have scored nearly 100 per cent. If not, then just go through all the shapes of the digits once more. It should not take more than five minutes to master all the corresponding shapes of the digits. Now let's see how this newly acquired knowledge can be handy in the following day-to-day situations.

**Situation 1:** Let's say you want to go shopping and complete some important tasks in the following order, from most important to least important.

1. Buying some chocolates for a kid's birthday in your neighbourhood.
2. Posting a letter.
3. Purchasing a mobile phone for your father.
4. Giving the pressure cooker for repairing.
5. Buying few kilos of potatoes.
6. Buying today's newspaper.

7. Buying one dozen bananas.

8. Buying soap.

9. Giving your bike for headlight repairing.

Now to remember the list without spending much time in memorising just decide to call number 1 a stick while you are thinking or reading or deciding the first task and simply associate things with it. So, here's how you could do it...

**For task 1:** Imagine a **stick** made up of **chocolates**.

With some practice, you will realize that simply by thinking of the corresponding shape of the digit, your brain will automatically suggest an appropriate association with the task at hand.

**For task 2:** A **duck** posting a **letter**.

**For task 3:** Your father has bought a **heart**-shaped **mobile phone** from the market.

1          2                    3

Spend three to four seconds imagining it colourfully before going to the next.

**For task 4:** A **pressure cooker** is lying on a **chair**.

**For task 5:** A big sack of **potatoes** is hanging on a **hook**.

**For task 6:** Today's **newspaper** headline has news about **hockey** Tournament.

**For task 7:** A vendor is selling **bananas** under a **lamp-post**.

**For task 8:** The student is washing spectacles with **soap**.

**For task 9:** Your friend has replaced the bike's **headlight** with a big round golden coloured **lollipop**.

Don't go back and revise even if you have not read the above explanation with the intention of memorising. Just take the following test:

### Test

To buy bananas was at:

a) Number 3

b) Number 4

c) Number 7

d) Number 1

The item at number 5 was:

a) Potatoes

b) Repairing head light of bike

c) Posting a letter

d) Bag of chocolates

Buying soap was at _____ number.

_____ was at 9th position.

Repairing the pressure cooker was at _____ position.

I can easily guess that you would have passed this test with flying colours. And that is the power of visualization. Now you are better equipped to correlate it with the Secret Memory Formula.

**Video File > Memory Leakage Control > Audio File**

Whatever may be the content for memorizing, focus on converting it into a video file as you already know it cannot leak, unlike an audio file. Now let's take another day-to-day situation.

**Situation 2:** Remembering and recalling everyday appointments.

Here, I am going to modify the Shape Method a bit so that it may suit this situation. I call it the **Memory Clock Method**.

As you memorized the shopping list in an order using the Shape Method, you may similarly use it to remember appointments also. Just consider:

1 o'clock: Stick
2 o'clock: Duck
3 o'clock: Heart
4 o'clock: Chair
5 o'clock: Hook
6 o'clock: Hockey
7 o'clock: Lamp-post

8 o'clock: Spectacles
9 o'clock: Lollipop
10 o'clock: Bat and ball
11 o'clock: Road
12 o'clock: Cap

You can associate the time (digit) with the corresponding shape and then with the task.

As I have discussed earlier, the most interesting thing about memory techniques is that they can be easily used in daily life, academic life, or professional life.

Let's take another situation:

**Situation 3:** Let's assume at the last moment before going for an exam, a student comes to know that a particular chapter or a particular question for which he has not prepared is expected in the examination.

For instance:

**Question:** What are the properties of plastic?

**Answer:** The properties of plastics are as follows:

1. Plastic has a low melting point.
2. Plastic is light in weight.
3. Plastic has the ability to take a variety of colours.
4. Plastic has transparency.
5. Plastic is corrosion resistant.
6. Plastics are good for thermal and electrical insulation.
7. Plastic has an adhesive property.
8. Plastic has a toughness quality.
9. Plastic can be easily moulded.
10. Plastic has low maintenance cost.
11. Plastic has low fabrication cost for shaping into desired

shaped products.
12. Plastic has decorative surface effects.
13. Plastic is chemically inert.
14. Plastic has low thermal expansion co-efficient capacity.
15. Plastic is impermeable to water.
16. Plastic is a good absorbent of vibrations and sound.
17. Plastic is excellent in finish.
18. Plastic has dimensional stability.
19. Plastic has high resistance to abrasion.
20. Plastic is insect resistant.

We have assumed in this situation that the student is running short of time and, at most, he can just take a quick glance at this answer before he enters the examination hall. To ensure that he retains most points in just one glance, he must imagine the shape of numbers corresponding to each of the points (digits). For example, he may visualize like this:

1. Plastic sticks are melting in the hot sun.
2. The ducks are made of plastic and light in weight.
3. A plastic heart is available in a variety of colours for Valentine's Day.
4. Your mother has bought a transparent plastic chair.
5. A plastic hook is corrosion resistant and available in the market now.
6. A hockey stick is thermally and electrically insulated since it has a plastic handle.
7. A plastic lamp-post can be fixed easily on the ground, because of its adhesive property.
8. Spectacles made of plastic are better as their toughness can be ensured.

9. Plastic lollipops can easily be chewed and is mouldable into many funny shapes.

10. Bat and ball sets made of plastic are very low maintenance.

11. Some labourers on the road are fabricating plastic in different shapes.

12. You and your friends are wearing caps with decorative surfaces made up of plastic.

Now, in the examination hall, the very thought of the shapes of the numbers, along with the visualizations, will help the student recall the exact details.

**Test**

Let's go for a test.

**What are the properties of plastic?**

(Think of the Shape Method with visualization and association in mind to recall the points learnt above.)

1. _____

2. _____

3. _____

4. _____

5. _____

6. _____

7. _____

8. _____

9. _____

10. _____

11. _____

12. _____

Now your question could be that the above answer contains twenty points, whereas, using the Shape Method, we are writing down just twelve.

Here at this point of learning memory techniques you must understand that according to your requirement you must extend and modify the memory codes and learning strategy so that it may fit your need and that a one-time effort will help you develop a system which will help you throughout.

For instance, in this case we can extend the Shape Method beyond twelve like this:

| | | |
|---|---|---|
| 13-Butterfly | 13 | |
| 14-Sailing Boat | 4 | |
| 15-Cigar and pipe | 15 | |

| | | |
|---|---|---|
| 16-Elephant's trunk | 16 | |
| 17-Bread Pakora | 17 | |
| 18-Hourglass | 18 | |
| 19-Compass | 19 | |

| 20-Scooter |  |
|---|---|

The above are my suggestions, but you may create your own personal Shape Method codes.

Once a code is created, it will last you a lifetime. You can use it in lots of situations; it will prove useful and can serve as an instant mental diary ready to accumulate urgent stuff.

However, this technique is more suitable when you need to remember some smaller and simpler groups of information, especially for a particular length of time—such as appointments or a shopping list. Once the task is completed, you do not need the memory of the information and the same Shape Method can be used for other purposes conveniently.

CHAPTER 3

-------------------------------------------------------------------------

# HOW TO MEMORIZE A DICTIONARY

WHILE MEMORIZING the dictionary, I used to think in pictures. Whenever I read a word unfamiliar to me, I would immediately translate it into a full-colour video file with sound and movements, which ran like a movie in my head. Then I would associate the video files of these unknown words with their meanings. When somebody would ask me the meaning of a word from my dictionary, it was already translated into a picture in my mind and I was able to recall it with ease.

Language-based thinkers may find this style difficult to understand, but in my job as a memory trainer, visual thinking is of tremendous value. Visual thinking helped me to store dictionary entries in my mind. I have a video library of words in my imagination.

Converting abstract words into lively pictures is an art. Here in this chapter you are going to learn my favourite simple yet powerful method—**the Word Image System (WIS),** to convert words into vivid, colourful images. The beauty of the method I use lies in its simplicity.

In the previous two chapters you might have enjoyed remembering things by imaging them in your mind. Whenever words like cap, toothpaste, mobile, bucket, chocolate, newspaper, potato etc., were required to be seen in your mind you visualized them promptly with no problem. You could do that since they were by default in video format as you have already seen or experienced them in your day-to-day life. However, words and concepts that we encounter in our social, professional or academic lives are not in a ready-to-imagine format but we are supposed to remember them as well.

Using WIS, we translate seemingly difficult to imagine words or ideas into interesting visuals or video files. For example, think of the word 'tectonic'. It is an adjective which means, 'pertaining to the earth's crust and the various forces affecting it'.

Can you visualize it? If this word is unknown to you, then you would not be able to visualize it. You do not have any problem visualizing the meaning of the word. But the word 'tectonic' in itself does not evoke any visual.

Following WIS, you need to think of a similar sounding video file for 'tectonic'. To get access to that, say it two or three times in your mind—'tectonic...tec-tonic...tec-tonic...'—and a similar-sounding word of phrase pops up in your mind, 'take tonic'. You might imagine that you are 'taking a tonic' for the word 'tectonic'. Now, your video file for the word 'tectonic' is 'taking a tonic'.

Now to remember the meaning of 'tectonic' link it by visualizing that you are taking a tonic (tectonic) 'to end a crusty feeling in your stomach' or any other image that you prefer as per the definition given in the paragraph above.

So, we use WIS to create a video file in our brain for an unknown word by linking it to something imaginable. Thus the recollection of one thing helps recall the other. Like in above example, when you hear 'tectonic' (unknown word) you recall 'taking a tonic' (video file) and then you reach to the meaning (crusty feeling) associated with it.

There can be many ways to convert an unknown word or phrase (audio file) to a video file but the strongest way is through senses, emotions, and the use of rhymes—and all of these form the basis of WIS.

To comprehend this let us take one more example, the word 'abase'.

Abase is a verb and means 'to humiliate or degrade'. Now just to tell you, you may think of other word images that work better for you than the ones provided in this book. That is all right, go ahead and use them. Here I give my word image for 'abase'.

**Word image for 'abase'**: Basement

**Think:** When you drag someone to a basement (abase) you 'humiliate or degrade' them.

Not only does WIS work for the English vocabulary or any other language, it can be applied to convert any word from any subject into an interesting video file. Though, in this chapter and next chapter I have taken examples from vocabulary and general knowledge, the applications of this method are many.

After completing this chapter and doing a few more words with WIS, many of the questions in your mind about the process will clear up. Nevertheless, keep the following two points in mind while using WIS.

**Step 1:** You can relate unknown words you want to remember, to the things and people that you know, by making up phrases or names that are very familiar and memorable to you. But these names and phrases must be imagined visually, i.e. in video file format.

**Step 2:** Then make up funny and emotional scenes (associations) in your head. The more absurd the imagined situation the greater the impact the image will have and the better will be the retention. Play with your imagination and have fun.

Let us practice some more with WIS. The words chosen here appear daily in newspapers, business magazines and in exams like GRE, TOEFL, CAT, Bank PO, etc.

Please note that WIS only helps you recall the meaning of the word. It does not make you proficient in its usage. So I have also given few examples showing how to use a memorized word. I would suggest that when you make your own vocabulary list and practice them by using WIS in sentences to command full mastery.

1. **Adroit:** adjective; 'clever or skilful'
   Android phones
   **Android** phones are **adroit** at helping you to use many apps.

**Sentences:**

• He was **adroit** at tax-avoidance.

I AM CLEVER AND SKILFUL AT
SOCIAL MEDIA, E-MAILS, CALLS, DIARY,
MAPS, APPS, BANKING AND BLAH BLAH
BLAH

- I thought that was amusing, but not particularly **adroit**.
- Many were also very **adroit** in terms of choosing a school.
- Proverbs aim to show a person how to become **adroit** at the greatest skill of all, the skill of living.
- The retailer showed **adroit** handling of the problem.

2. **Aghast:** adjective; 'filled with horror or shock'
   A ghost

The boy stood **aghast** at the sight of **a ghost**.

**Sentences:**

- He stood **aghast** at the terrible sight.
- They were **aghast** at her bad behaviour.
- He was **aghast** at the shocking news.
- The robbers stood **aghast** at the sudden appearance of the policemen.
- Susan looked **aghast** at her son's report card.

3. **Belie:** verb; 'to misrepresent or expose something as false'
Bee-lie

The bee lied to the bear in order to belie the honey she kept in the beehive.

**Sentences:**

- His cheerful manner **belied** his real feelings.

- His angelic looks **belie** his character.
- He spoke roughly in order to **belie** his air of gentility.
- At first glance, life at the boarding school seemed to **belie** all the bad things I had heard about it.
- Their laughter **belied** their grieving hearts.

4. **Bucolic:** adjective; 'rural, rustic'
   Bull colic

Farm surroundings are **bucolic**, but this **bull** often gets **colic** here.

**Sentences:**

- Its unique architecture, winding streets and **bucolic** setting make it a great getaway.
- This year's October festival was a jolly, **bucolic** spectacle.

- It's true that I had a **bucolic**, peaceful childhood, growing up in a house next to our family orchard.
- The cows grazing nearby add to the farm's **bucolic** charm.
- Summer turns to winter in this rhyming counting book, the **bucolic** illustrations of which have a pleasingly old-fashioned look and feel.

5. **Cacophony:** adjective; 'a harsh inharmonious sound'
   Cough on phone

The **cacophony** of sound on the **phone** was due to my uncle's **cough**.

**Sentences:**

- These form a wonderful crazy **cacophony** which works amazingly well.
- I heard a **cacophony** of horns during the traffic jam.
- We were greeted by a **cacophony** of sound as we entered the road.
- The dogs in our neighbourhood create a **cacophony** that wakes me up every morning.
- The **cacophony** in the crowded classroom drowned out the principal's announcement.

6. **Chary:** adjective; 'very cautious'
   Cherry

BE CAUTIOUS WITH UNRIPE CHERRIES

The gardener is **chary** of plucking unripe **cherries** from the tree.

**Sentences:**

- The mountaineer was **chary** about taking any foolish risk.
- Nearly all people are quick to censure but rather **chary** to praise.
- But even while they were covering the event, some at the networks were **chary**.
- Rahul is very **chary** about investing. He would rather be content with the money he has than take the risk of investing it in stocks and shares and losing it.
- Having been repulsed by his first girlfriend when he proposed to her, Sid is **chary** of doing any such thing again.

7. **Decorous:** adjective; 'well-behaved'
   The chorus

Singers in the **chorus** are not rebels; they are **decorous**.

**Sentences:**

- However deadly his deeds, his language is always **decorous**.
- The language may be more **decorous** today, but the ideas are the same.
- This most **decorous** of men could barely oblige; tears rolled down his face.
- The slowdown since then has been equally **decorous**.
- It was a spectacularly **decorous** event, if such a thing is possible.

8. **Despot:** noun; 'an all-powerful ruler'
   The spot

HA HA HA SEE THE SPOTS

The king whose robe had **the** blood **spot** is a **despot**.

**Sentences:**

- They'll even protect a **despot** if it is in their interest, no care for human rights.
- We rely on an enlightened **despot** to preserve our future.
- His father, whom he calls a **despot**, forbade it.
- Both men were **despots**, in their different ways.
- You are a benevolent **despot**.

9. **Encumber:** verb; 'to hinder or restrict motion'
   Cucumber

Carrying the big **cucumber encumbered** the boy so much, that he was unable to walk with it very far.

**Sentences:**

- He said the campaign did not encumber the public funds in any way.
- The fact that there are so many people from different political orientations should enhance the debate, not **encumber** it.
- Women make more journeys using public transport, with children and otherwise **encumbered.**
- They were **encumbered** by the large amount of luggage they carried on their journeys.
- Young schoolchildren are **encumbered** by the heavy bags they have to carry every day to school.

**10. Enervate:** adjective; 'lacking in energy or vitality'
Energy waste

Rahul plays all day, **wastes** his **energy** and later feels **enervated** when it is time to study.

**Sentences:**

- The wolf's plan of attack was to **enervate** the buffalo and kill it.

- The alcohol appeared to **enervate** Rajiv's ability to focus at work.
- The doctors were **enervated** at the end of the fifteen-hour operation.
- The passengers were **enervated** at the end of the long flight.
- When the soldiers put dynamite under the bridge, they hoped it would **enervate** the foundation to the point of collapse.

11. **Evanescent:** adjective; 'soon passing out of sight, memory, or existence'
Eva's scent

**Eva's scent** filled the room for a few moments and then became **evanescent**.

**Sentences:**

- Rainbows are **evanescent** because they do not stay around for long periods of time.
- When the temperature rises, the snow becomes **evanescent** as it turns into water.
- The lightning was **evanescent** and disappeared just as quickly as it appeared.
- Unfortunately, the best dreams are always **evanescent** and end at sunrise.
- Money is **evanescent**, but love and friendship are forever.

12. **Fastidious:** adjective; 'very particular or choosy, very concerned with details, hard to please'
    Fast-TDS (TDS means 'tax deducted at source')

OH, I HAVE TO BE VERY METICULOUS
WITH DETAILS FOR TDS RETURNS

Our boss is very **fastidious** and is calculating the **TDS meticulously.**

**Sentences:**

- My aunt was a **fastidious** woman who bathed thrice a day.
- **Fastidious** to a fault, the diva made no friends on her music tour.
- While Harish would eat just about anything, his wife was so **fastidious** she barely ate anything.
- Constantly licking themselves clean, cats are **fastidious** creatures.
- You will have few friends if you do not change your habit of being so **fastidious**.

13. **Fatuous:** adjective; 'silly and pointless, lacking intelligence'
    Fat

By ignoring the signs, the **fat, fatuous** runner fell into a hole.

**Sentences:**

- Buying a car without negotiating the price is a **fatuous** move.
- It was a **fatuous** choice to carry so many glasses at once.
- My brother was **fatuous** enough to sprint across the wet kitchen floor.
- The misuse of big words in his campaign speech made the politician sound **fatuous**.
- The football player's **fatuous** move caused his team to lose the game.

**14. Garrulous:** adjective; 'talkative, usually about unimportant things'
Gorilla

This **garrulous gorilla** loves to come to parties, but Jane does not seem to be very fond of his company.

**Sentences:**

- Desperate for peace and quiet, the teacher shouted 'Shut up!' to calm his **garrulous** students.
- Mom, who is usually loud and **garrulous**, was surprisingly quiet as a mouse this morning.
- Because Richa is **garrulous**, asking her to keep a secret is impossible.
- My **garrulous** sister talks on the phone all day.
- **Garrulous** people make great talk show hosts.

**15. Gregarious:** adjective; 'enjoying the company of others; outgoing or social'
Group-carry-us

**NOW WE CAN ENJOY THEIR COMPANY**

The two friends were stranded but when their **group came to carry** them they had a **gregarious** time once again.

**Sentences:**

- **Gregarious** people are likely to hang out with friends every weekend while reserved people keep to themselves.
- If you want to be more approachable, show a **gregarious** smile.
- Storms of people rushed in the nightclub to have a **gregarious** time dancing and singing to the music.
- As **gregarious** as you are with me, I am sure everyone will admire you.
- You do not typically associate nerdy computer programmers of having a **gregarious** personality.

16. **Hone:** verb; 'to sharpen; to make something perfect and more suitable'
Horn

**I AM HONING MY HORNS**

The goat **hones** its **horns** on a stone to make them sharp.

**Sentences:**

- It took him about fifteen years to **hone** his skills.
- Anuradha could be a compelling novelist—if only she would **hone** her storytelling techniques.
- The team is still trying to **hone** the method.
- Presenting concepts realistically may improve learning, and **hone** other skills as well.
- Insurers have to **hone** their investment-management skills if they are to compete in this new environment.

**17. Inane:** adjective; 'devoid of intelligence, senseless'
Insane

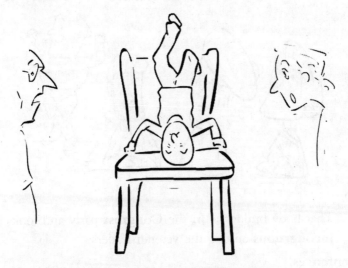

That **inane** boy is acting **insane**.

**Sentences:**

- Even though Seema is a math genius, she acts **inane** in class because she likes getting extra attention.

- Your idea about eating plastic fruit is totally **inane**.
- Although Rishabh has a college degree, he still behaves in an **inane** manner at times.
- That weird movie about the robotic vampires is one of the most **inane** films I have ever seen!
- My teacher is really good at ignoring **inane** comments from the clowns in our class.

**18. Incongruous:** adjective; 'lacking in harmony or appropriateness'
In Congress

INCONGRUOUS MAN IN CONGRESS

That body builder is **in** the **Congress** party and looks **incongruous** among the veteran leaders.

**Sentences**:

- How **incongruous**! My fat doctor telling me to lose weight!
- Wearing a raincoat in sunny weather is quite **incongruous**.

- There's something **incongruous** about eating dessert before the main course.
- Try mixing water and oil and you will see an **incongruous** blend.
- The statement you gave yesterday was **incongruous** with the witness' testimony.

**19. Indolent:** adjective; 'lazy'
Indian land

People are generally **indolent** on **Indian land**.

**Sentences**:

- Jackson lost his job because he was an **indolent** employee who did nothing but sleep at his desk all day.
- My **indolent** daughter waited until the last possible day to start her lengthy research paper.
- The fact Alia never got up before noon told everyone she was an **indolent** person.
- Rather than fetch the ball, the **indolent** dog decided to take a nap.
- Katrina was an **indolent** girl who never completed her chores.

**20. Intractable:** adjective; 'hard to control or deal with'
Tractor

The farmer could not finish his work because of the **intractable tractor**.

**Sentences:**

- The teacher was having trouble with the new student who was being **intractable**.
- It was a brilliant solution to what had been an **intractable** problem.
- Good medical treatment can help people with even those illnesses that seem **intractable**.
- He proved **intractable** and refused to listen to reason.
- Now as then, the same **intractable** questions were avoided and in the end successfully evaded.

**21. Lachrymose:** adjective; 'tearful, sad'
Lack the most

I LACK THE MOST

The poor girl who **lacked the most** became **lachrymose**.

**Sentences:**

- After her husband died, my aunt became a **lachrymose** woman who couldn't stop crying.
- When I watch television shows about people dying from cancer, I become very **lachrymose**.
- The pictures of the dead children made everyone **lachrymose** and sad.
- I rarely cry so you should definitely not be calling me **lachrymose**!
- The funeral home was filled with **lachrymose** mourners.

**22. Lionize**: adjective; 'treat as a celebrity'.
Lion

The **lion** was **lionized** by the media after his recent hit movie.

**Sentences:**

- He was admired by the communists, but **lionized** by nationalists.
- His face has appeared on posters and he has been **lionized** by the media.
- He **lionized** the writer as a free individual striving for objective truth.
- "Armenians aren't human," another said, when I suggested that a murderer was being **lionized**.
- The rich man was lionised, though he was really nothing more than a thief.

**23. Malevolent:** adjective; 'having or showing a wish to do evil to others'
Male is violent

A **malevolent male** is **violent** with his wife.

**Sentences:**

- How **malevolent** of you to wish that I was dead!
- Seeing the **malevolent** look on the man's face, Leena knew she was in danger.
- How can you date a man who has such a **malevolent** past?
- Because of their **malevolent** purposes, hand grenades are not allowed on commercial flights.
- She was evil and **malevolent.**

**24. Melancholic:** adjective; 'sadness or depression'
Melon colic

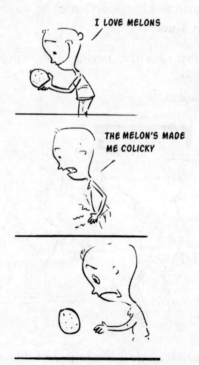

Bhanu suffers from **colic** every time he eats a **melon,** and this makes him **melancholic.**

**Sentences**:

- We became **melancholic** at the film's tragic ending.
- After Sheetal broke up with her fiancée, she walked around **melancholic** for weeks.
- Not surprisingly, after the death of her husband, Zeenat was extremely **melancholic**.
- There is nothing more **melancholic** than a young child's funeral.
- He writes the most **melancholic** music!

**25. Nadir:** noun; 'the lowest point, worst moment'
No door

The situation reached its **nadir** when the boy chased by the bull reached a house but found **no** one opening the **door**!

**Sentences:**

- This spiritual **nadir** came as his career began to peak.
- At the **nadir**, I was sleeping about two or three hours a night and writing or revising when everyone else was asleep.
- The usage is as much as three times higher at its peak than at its **nadir**.
- It was, I felt, the **nadir** of masculinity.
- Finally, we come to the **nadir** of contemporary bad manners.

**26. Obfuscate:** verb; 'to make something more difficult to understand'
Office cat

WHY THIS CAT IN OFFICE?

The boss further **obfuscated** the situation by bringing his **cat** to the **office** to keep an eye on the employees.

**Sentences:**

- Because I am a sympathetic teacher, I avoid using language which will **obfuscate** my students.
- The efforts of the translator only served to **obfuscate** an already confusing conversation.
- The last thing I want to do is **obfuscate** the concept by trying to explain it too rapidly.
- Because I am honest, I never try to **obfuscate** my true intentions!
- His manhandling the evidence served to **obfuscate** matters for the police when they reached the crime scene.

**27. Opulent:** adjective; 'rich and wealthy'
Opals

**Opulent** women wear **opals**.

**Sentences:**

- The wedding was so **opulent** and lavish.
- Don't judge him by his shabby clothes, he owns an **opulent** mansion in a posh area of the city.
- The party was too **opulent** and gaudy for my taste.
- She better find herself a wealthy husband who is able to support her **opulent** lifestyle.
- His **opulent** friends influenced his lifestyle so much that he started going against his poor parents for not giving him enough money.

**28. Parsimony:** adjective; 'extreme unwillingness to spend money'

Purse of money

My mother was very parsimonious despite having a **purse** full **of money.**

**Sentences:**

- To save money, the **parsimonious** man bought used clothes.
- My mother is **parsimonious** and never tips more than five per cent.
- Even though I have plenty of money, I tend to be **parsimonious** with my spending.
- Since my grandmother is on a fixed income, she is **parsimonious** and clips every coupon she sees.
- Despite his wealth, the **parsimonious** millionaire refused to give any money to charity.

**29. Petulant:** adjective; 'bad tempered, rude or impatient'

Pet

MY PET IS SO PETULANT

No one liked the **petulant pet**.

**Sentences:**

- He was a **petulant** child who was aggravated by the smallest things.
- When the movie started, the **petulant** infant would not stop crying because of the loud noise.
- My oldest sister is a **petulant** woman who complains constantly.
- Because she whined about everything on the movie set, the studio head described the actress as **petulant**.
- While I can be a bit moody, I am not **petulant** because I do not let small issues get to me.

**30. Placate:** verb; 'to soothe, prevent anger'
Play cat

IT SOOTHES MY ANGER

Humiliated by his mother's scolding, Monu started **playing** with **a cat** to **placate** his anger.

**Sentences:**

- She sensed nothing she could say would **placate** him.
- I don't need you to **placate** me!
- Maybe the need to **placate** his father had spawned the decision to call off the divorce.
- The airline gave out free drinks in an effort to **placate** angry travellers.
- One of the soldiers came over and tried to **placate** them both.

31. **Quixotic:** adjective; 'extremely idealistic; unrealistic and impractical'

    Queen-exotic

DON'T BE SO QUIXOTIC!

The **quixotic queen** wants **exotic things only** and is very difficult to please.

**Sentences:**

- Although Mungerilal's plan for killing the giant was **quixotic**, it was the village's only hope.
- Henry knew running for class president was a **quixotic** idea, but he was not going to let his enemy run unopposed.
- It is **quixotic** to think you can get away with walking into the prison and breaking out your boyfriend.
- Everyone told Jennifer her dream of being a Hollywood star was **quixotic**, but she proved them wrong when she became a ten million dollar actress.
- Nobody believed the weak-looking boy would achieve his **quixotic** goal of making the football team.

32. **Raconteur:** noun; 'storyteller'
Re-encounter
Billu's neighbour is a **raconteur** by nature and if you **re-encounter** him, he always insists on recounting some story.

**Sentences:**

- Most good film directors are known to be naturally gifted **raconteurs** too.
- There's no **raconteur** like my grandmother. The way she narrates stories is so lifelike.
- She is a skilled **raconteur** and she uses this ability to convince people.
- When good **raconteurs** narrate stories, they add a lot of emotion and expression to make it engrossing.

- He is not just a linguist and professor of English, but also an awesome **raconteur** who spins beautiful yarns out of simple words.

**33. Reticent:** adjective; 'not revealing one's thoughts or feelings'
Rat-scent

Whenever this rat wants to act **reticent** he puts on **rat-scent.**

**Sentences:**

- Babita likes to discuss her personal life with our co-workers, but I am much more **reticent.**

- Rather than voice her political opinions, Esha prefers to remain **reticent**.
- When asked if he broke the lamp, the child was **reticent** and refused to make eye contact.
- Jagat was **reticent** when I asked why he did not go to school yesterday.
- It is okay to be **reticent** around people you do not know well.

34. **Retrograde:** adjective; 'directed or moving backwards'
    Grades

Instead of helping the children improve, the new teacher had a **retrograde** effect on their marks!

**Sentences:**

- Perhaps he is unaware that this is a **retrograde** move.
- It is cowardly of him to **retrograde** in face of danger.
- It also had a **retrograde** view of career women.
- The people who are fighting us are a bunch of **retrograde** medievalists.
- Academic standards have **retrograded**.

35. **Salutary:** adjective; 'beneficial'
    Salute

SALUTES ARE ALWAYS SALUTARY    YOU GOT A PROMOTION

**Salutes** to the boss are always **salutary**.

**Sentences:**

- We're not suggesting that this recipe has **salutary** effects, but it is delicious.
- The leaf of the neem tree can prove **salutary** in various chronic conditions.
- The museum is a **salutary** reminder of what life was like in the past.
- The principal's warning had a **salutary** effect on the naughty students.
- His return has had a **salutary** effect on the whole office.

**36. Sanguine:** adjective; 'optimistic, cheerful'
Penguin

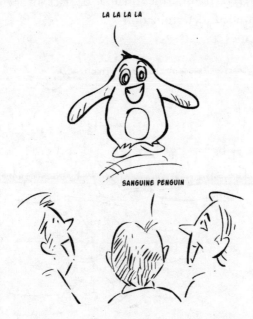

The children were amused to see a **sanguine penguin**.

**Sentences:**

- Although the economy is looking up, we should still not be too **sanguine** about the future.
- You can tell by the big smile on her face that she has a **sanguine** temperament!
- Despite the fact the soldiers have not been home in eight months, they are still **sanguine** about seeing their families soon.
- The bank manager did not feel **sanguine** about recovering the loan.
- Even though the company was closing stores, its shareholders were **sanguine** about their future earnings.

37. **Tenacity:** noun; 'the quality or fact of being very determined; determination'
Ten cities

TENACIOUS ENOUGH TO CROSS TEN CITIES

The boy showed great **tenacity** by running across **ten cities** non-stop.

**Sentences:**

- Our show, at its core, is really about the **tenacity** of the human spirit.
- These people were worthy of love and admiration in their blind loyalty, in their blind strength and **tenacity**.
- One can admire Gyan for his **tenacity** and hard work in the midst of tremendously trying circumstances.
- Success is the product of hard work, **tenacity** and patience.
- Babies show a great deal of **tenacity** in learning to walk and talk.

38. **Ungainly:** adjective; 'awkward; clumsy'.
    Game

This old car is so **ungainly** for the **game**.

**Sentences**:

- I had found the dress to be **ungainly** and very badly stitched.
- This is an **ungainly** bridge.
- The tall, **ungainly** girl left the hall.
- The designs have been criticised for their **ungainly** look.
- The furniture looked heavy and **ungainly**.

**39. Voluble:** adjective; 'talking with ease'
Volleyball

The **voluble volleyball** players continued talking for hours in spite of the coach's warning.

**Sentences**:

- Where he is **voluble** and rude, she measures her words.
- Roma is so **voluble** that there is no fear of her hiding her opinions.

- Viewers were equally **voluble** on the subject of the badly presented Awards show.
- I talked to a **voluble** young man working for one of the few open vendors.
- Two groups have formed—one increasingly **voluble** in their criticism of the manager, one fiercely supportive.

**40. Zealot:** noun; 'fanatic; a person who shows great enthusiasm for a cause'
Zeal lot

WOHOO...I HAVE DONE IT!

A **zealot** has a lot of **zeal**.

**Sentences:**
- The religious **zealot** was willing to break the law.
- The **zealot** walked over a thousand miles to get people to sign his petition.

- Some people **call** Peter a **zealot**.
- The cult leader was a **zealot** who killed anyone who dared to question his principles.
- When the **zealot** wrote his memoirs, he wrote that he fought all his wars for his god.

# CHAPTER 4

## HOW TO MEMORIZE GENERAL KNOWLEDGE

IF SOMEONE asks you to memorize the name of countries and their capitals, how would you do it? It's really simple with the Word Image System (WIS). For instance, take 'Bulgaria'. First come up with a similar sounding word: 'Bull-Gurr'. Think of this as a **bull** saying **'gurr'**.

The capital of Bulgaria (your bull saying 'gurr'!) is Sofia. Using WIS the picture of 'Sofa' comes to the mind. Now how can you characterize the above two images in a movie to memorize it? Just think of the **bull** sleeping on a sofa and snoring **'gurr'**, **'gurr'**. With this video file you have learned the information that 'Sofia' is the capital of 'Bulgaria'. But someone may object that even if we recall the sofa and bull together how can we interpret that this picture indicates that Sofia is the capital of Bulgaria? What if somebody thinks that Sofia is the currency or parliament of Bulgaria? For this you may makeover the bull a little bit in your video file, **put a cap on his head** to imply that it is capital (cap) and not something else.

Similarly in case of remembering currencies introduce 'currency notes' in the middle of your associations while visualizing a film, and so on for parliament or languages, etc. Since you are the director/producer of the video files, you may imagine anything that makes you recall correctly and speedily. The only limit is your imagination. In forthcoming chapters you will see that even complex chemical equations and biological terms can be easily remembered with this method. The WIS brings you so close to your answers that there is no further scope of confusion.

Let us have a look at the visuals of some of the abstract words based on WIS.

Germany/Germ-many/many germs
Iran/I-ran/I am running
Israel/Is-reel/thread reel is rolling
Spain/S-pain/severe pain
Sweden/Swe-den/sweet-den/a den of sweets
Denmark/Den-mark/a den with lot of marks

See how we have broken these words and derived new imaginable words out of them. Now let us try and break the names of the parliaments of these countries. For example the German parliament is called the 'Bundestag'. Break this into Bun-des-tag/bun the tag.

You may imagine a scene at a parliament where leaders are given a bun to eat; each **bun** has **the tag** (Bun-des-tag) with the leader's name. As they bite in, they find the buns have many germs (Germ-many).

You should make your associations larger than life; to

exaggerate the above you may further imagine that the germs are creeping out of buns and onto the leaders' hands.

Follow these steps while converting and associating simple words (could be names of countries/cities; could be concepts/objects etc.) into visuals using the WIS method to get maximum benefit. To recap:

**Step 1:** Break up the word (for instance, as we saw, Germany became germ-many).

**Step 2:** Assign images to words. If you happen to have a personal memory associated with the word/concept/object, recall that and fit it into your mental video. For example, I have visited Dubai many times, and I think of the well-known skyscraper Burj Khalifa whenever I need to imagine Dubai. I associate Dubai with Burj Khalifa because I have personal memories of the place. Similarly you could also think of something real that reminds you of the non-visual thing, be it a place or person.

So you have flexibility to convert a word, concept or idea into a visual by exploring your real life experiences associated with it. Make a deliberate effort to avoid dull pictorial images. Be careful to select something visual to represent the main idea—thinking in terms of substitute abstract ideas for already non-visual main words may lead to inability to recollect them later.

**Step 3:** Beside main associations there could be peripheral information that may be equally important. For example, while associating Germany with Bundestag, you also needed to tag in your mind that Bundestag is the parliament of Germany. Otherwise you could be confused about whether it was the capital or the currency or something else. You might have noticed that we removed this confusion in the above example by visualizing the **leaders in a parliament** eating buns. We knowingly visualized parliament to ascertain that this association is to remember the parliament.

And also please notice that in case of the mental video on Bulgaria and Sofia you placed a **cap** on the bull's head to remind yourself that this association indicates the capital. So rule of the thumb is, chalk out the confusion and make a strategy to remove it in your imagination.

Let us look at another example: the first aeroplane was invented by the Wright Brothers.

The non-visual or audio word here is 'Wright Brothers'. You can imagine the video file like this: two brothers have made an aeroplane for the first time and are very cautious before taking-off. So they are checking the plane meticulously and marking a right (√, Wright) on every part they have checked. To add emotions and excitement to this video visualize that people are gathered outside to see how the first aeroplane would fly. They are cheering the Wright Brothers by shouting: 'You are the right brothers! We are proud of you.'

Now you will never forget that the first aeroplane was invented by the Wright Brothers. By doing this you have actually converted simple boring information into an interesting, exciting, emotional video file with the help of WIS.

Any similar information can be tackled in the same way. Suppose you need to memorize the names of books and their authors—for instance, *Geetanjali* written by Rabindranath Tagore. You can imagine and link the books and authors like this:

### *Gitanjali* and **Rabindranath Tagore:**

(Bhagavad) Gita–anjali (Hindi word meaning 'handful')

Rabindranath Tagore is holding the Bhagavad Gita in his anjali, indicating that he wrote *Gitanjali*.

### **H.G. Wells and *The Time Machine*:**

Well

H.G. Wells is sitting on a well to finish his book before time runs out, indicating he wrote the book *The Time Machine*.

### *Hamlet and Shakespeare:*

Helmet

Shakespeare is writing a book wearing a helmet.

Now let's look at how to memorize the names of inventors and inventions.

### Alexander Graham Bell and the telephone:

Alexander wearing bells.

Here you need to visualize that Alexander, who is wearing bells, is assembling a telephone, indicating his invention.

Now it is time for you to practise mastering the method. Please try to remember on your own the following facts using **Word Image and Association Method (WIAM).**

## Exercise 1

| Country | Capital | Your Word Image |
|---|---|---|
| 1. Afghanistan | Kabul | ................................. |
| 2. Albania | Tirane | ................................. |
| 3. Angola | Luanda | ................................. |
| 4. Armenia | Yerevan | ................................. |
| 5. Australia | Canberra | ................................. |
| 6. Azerbaijan | Baku | ................................. |
| 7. Bahrain | Manama | ................................. |
| 8. Belgium | Brussels | ................................. |
| 9. Bhutan | Thimphu | ................................. |
| 10. Canada | Ottawa | ................................. |

## Exercise 2

| Country | Currency | Your Word Image |
|---|---|---|
| Afghanistan | Afghani | ................................. |
| Albania | Lek | ................................. |
| Algeria | Dinar | ................................. |
| Andorra | Euro | ................................. |

## Exercise 3

| Country | Parliament | Your Word Image |
|---|---|---|
| Afghanistan | Shora | ................................. |
| Australia | Parliament | ................................. |
| Bangladesh | Jatia Parliament | ................................. |
| Denmark | Folketing | ................................. |
| Egypt | People's Assembly | ................................. |

# CHAPTER 5

---

# THE JOURNEY METHOD

PEOPLE WITH extraordinary memory abilities prove that that capacity of the human mind to store and reproduce is enormous. Some people are gifted, while others can acquire these skills through hard work and practice. One sophisticated technique that can make you a 'memory genius' is the **Journey Method**.

The Journey Method is a 7000-year old memory tool that was used by Greek and Roman speakers to remember long speeches, with surprising accuracy. They did it to prove that their memory abilities were beyond the normal range as they had special brains! In this chapter you will learn the same technique and then it is for you to decide whether we really need extraordinary brains to remember the things they did.

## What is the Journey Method?

The Journey Method provides you an effective platform based on the idea of remembering landmarks on a well-known route in a sequence.

You can use the Journey Method by linking information with landmarks on a well-known journey. This could, for example, be your journey to work in the morning; the route in your house from kitchen to bathroom; the way to visit your parents; or a tour around your nearest market. Once you are accustomed to the method in real life routes, you may be able to create imaginary journeys in your mind later.

To use this method effectively, you should prepare your journey in advance. Developing a journey in advance makes sure that all the landmarks are clear in your mind and you can confidently attach your information to them. First note down your journey, then visualize it again, and finally try to recall all the stops without referring to your written list.

Revise this two to three times mentally to perfect it.

To remember a list of items, speeches, experiments, historical events or question–answer points, all you need to do is to link them with the landmarks or stops on your journey. This method enables you to memorize long information easily and perfectly with sequence. You just need to create a journey long enough to match the length of your information to be remembered. You can remember the Periodic Table, lists of kings, prime ministers and presidents, names of states, geographical information or a long digit number for a memory feat.

Initially create smaller journeys but later you should

create a longer journey with a lot of landmarks.

This method is very handy in recalling information backwards or forwards or from any landmark within the journey.

The Journey Method is a powerful instrument in transforming your memory. This method gives your mind a reason to record the information you want to remember. Let us see the preparation and application of the Journey Method.

## Sample Journey 1

This is your first journey so let us start it with your home. Visualize your room as you can remember the journey created here easily. You must follow a logical path from start to finish, so choose objects in your room in a clockwise or anti-clockwise direction. To perform the journey in a uniform direction is important so that you can remember the sequence or order of the objects. These objects will work as memory journey 'stops' or hooks where you can hang the information you want to memorize. Let us consider a clockwise direction here.

Probably your room consists of the shown objects. Have a look at them carefully once again. Can you still visualize them with your eyes closed? Of course you can, as this is the place where you live. Going from sofa to exercise bike will create a room journey. Count the landmarks or stops in this journey. They are ten in number, so it is a ten-stop journey which can be used to remember any list of information up to ten points.

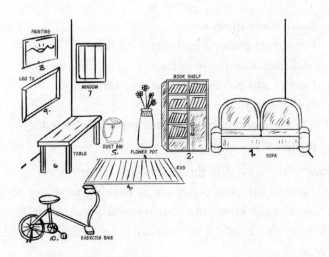

## Speech with Journey 1

Let us consider a real life situation where you have been given an election ticket by a leading political party and you are asked to deliver a speech on the party manifesto at a big gathering. But the problem is that you don't remember the manifesto. And you know that it will create a very good impression on your party colleagues and the public if you could speak without any notes.

Quickly glance at the ten-point manifesto of your newly joined party:

1. All BPL families to get rice or wheat every month at ₹2 per kg.
2. Ensure bank loan to farmers.
3. Generate employment through massive public spending on infrastructure projects.
4. Free and clean water.

5. Boost tourism sector.
6. Improving public healthcare facilities.
7. More security for women.
8. Protect and promote forests and forestation.
9. End corruption.
10. Create sports infrastructure, especially in educational institutions.

Now, you know that the manifesto of your party is new information for you, but there is nothing to worry about as you already know the journey you prepared at home. You have five minutes to memorize the manifesto handed over to you.

Let's memorize this manifesto with the help of your home journey.

1. The first point in the manifesto is that BPL families will get rice or wheat at the rate of ₹2 per kg.
   The first stop in your journey is the 'sofa'. Imagine that you are sitting on the sofa and distributing rice and wheat to poor people. To make it more catchy add pain to it by imagining poor people extremely pale and haggard.
2. The second point in your manifesto is ensuring bank loans to farmers.
   The second object in your journey is 'bookshelf'. Imagine a huge bookshelf with a signboard reading 'Bank'. Farmers are standing there and a clerk sitting on the bookshelf is approving their loans.
3. The third point in your manifesto is to generate employment.
   Link this point with the third stop in your journey

which is 'flower pot'. Imagine that many people have been provided employment to clean and maintain the mammoth-sized flower pot.

4. The fourth point in the manifesto is free and clean water. Connect the fourth point with the fourth stage in your journey which is 'rug'. Imagine that the dhobi is washing your dirty rug with clean water for free.

5. The fifth point in the manifesto is boosting the tourism sector.
   Think that you are leading a cleanliness campaign by placing 'dustbins' at different corners as hygiene will improve the chances of attracting tourists.

6. The sixth point is improving public healthcare.
   The sixth stop in your journey is 'table'. Imagine that your table is not just a table but has suddenly transformed into a 'treatment table' used in hospitals. Doctors are treating patients lying on the treatment table.

7. The seventh point is women's security.
   The seventh stop is the 'window' in your journey. Visualize that a woman is sitting at the window and two security guards are standing to safeguard her.

8. The eighth point is to protect and promote forests.
   The eighth stop is 'painting'. Think that your painting is one of a forest so lively that you can even hear the chirping of birds!

9. The ninth point is to end corruption.
   Imagine that anti-corruption movement 'LED' by Anna Hazare is being broadcast live on your LED TV.

10. The tenth point is creation of sports infrastructure in schools.

You have created sports infrastructure in schools by installing 'stationary bikes' for the students. Imagine students sitting and exercising on the stationary bike in your room.

This test will help you to practice. Fill the blanks.

1. ....................................................
2. ....................................................
3. ....................................................
4. ....................................................
5. ....................................................
6. ....................................................
7. ....................................................
8. ....................................................
9. ....................................................
10. ...................................................

## Sample Journey 2

How frequently do you go to the nearby market for shopping? Almost daily! So why not make a journey here too to help you memorize important information. Suppose the images of the landmarks shown in the picture are clear in your mind when you happen to pass through the market. The ten landmarks in your market journey are:

1. Your home
2. Parking
3. Bank
4. Sweet Shop

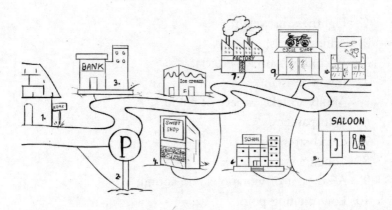

5.  Ice cream shop
6.  School
7.  Factory
8.  Salon
9.  Cycle shop
10. Restaurant

Revise this journey several times mentally; then take a pen and paper and jot it down. Is it the same as the original journey? If yes, then you are ready to go.

### Sample Journey 2

You had memorized the properties of plastic in Chapter 2 using the Shape Method. But there is no hard and fast rule of applying a particular method to particular information. The same content can be remembered with different techniques.

Let us take the same example once more, but this time we shall memorize it using the Journey Method.

1. Lightness in weight.
2. Adhesiveness.
3. Decorative surface effects.
4. Insect resistant.
5. Ability to take variety of colours.
6. Transparency.
7. Good strength.
8. Toughness.
9. Absorbent of vibrations and sound.
10. Low melting point.

| Stop Number | Journey stops | Property of plastic | Imaginary association |
|---|---|---|---|
| Stop 1. | Home | Lightness in weight | Your home has become light, so light like a balloon that it is tied to a string. And you need to reach the door using a staircase. To make this association strong, visualize yourself baffled as you do not know how to climb up to your home. |

| Stop 2. | Parking | Adhesiveness | Your bicycle is glued with an adhesive to the tarmac to park it. In fact all other vehicles are also stuck to the ground. |
|---------|---------|--------------|-----------------------------------------------|
| Stop 3. | Bank | Decorative surface effects | When you enter the bank you see designer plastic covers on the floor (surface) of the bank. Add strength to your association by visualizing that everybody is happy looking at the floor. |
| Stop 4. | Sweet Shop | Ability to take variety of colours | All the sweets are made of plastic and in a variety of colours. The shopkeeper is convincing people that these sweets are better as they are very beautiful in colour. |
| Stop 5. | Ice cream shop | Insect resistant | Insects are kept out because the ice cream has made the shop insect resistant. |

| Stop 6. | School | Transparency | All the classrooms have transparent plastic walls. You can see students studying there. |
| Stop 7. | Factory | Good strength | Factory workers are producing strong plastic sheets. They are trying to break them with a hammer but are unable to do so. |
| Stop 8. | Salon | Toughness | You are at the salon for a haircut. But the barber fails to cut your hair as it is too tough for his scissors. |
| Stop 9. | Cycle Shop | Absorbent of vibrations and sound | The mechanic is fixing a plastic bell that absorbs sound instead of making it. When you ring the bell it makes no sound. |
| Stop 10. | Restaurant | Low melting point | The restaurant serves food made of plastic that melts very fast when a cook starts heating it as it has a low melting point. |

Try to recall the properties of plastic with the help of Journey 2.

1. .......................................................
2. .......................................................
3. .......................................................
4. .......................................................
5. .......................................................
6. .......................................................
7. .......................................................
8. .......................................................
9. .......................................................
10. .......................................................

## Sample Journey 3

With all these examples, you must have understood the Journey Method and you must have also comprehended one more important thing—we were trying to convert audio files to video files. Using the Journey Method, you converted your information to video files and that is how you were ultimately able to retain the information so well. The Journey Method is not just restricted to a familiar locations with actual landmarks, it can be extended to any of your favourite or routine processes.

For instance, making tea; you may have made tea several times a day for many years. It can become one of your journeys. In the tea-preparation process, I use a few simple steps:

1. Take a vessel.

2. Add water to it.
3. Put it on the stove.
4. Add tea leaves.
5. Add sugar.
6. Add milk.
7. Serve it in a cup.

Now these steps can become a good memorable journey and prove very handy in learning important data. For example, suppose you want to learn the causes of heart failure. There are seven most important causes.

1. Stiffness of muscles.  **Vessel**
   Stiffness of muscles is the first cause and 'vessel' is the first stop of your tea preparation journey. Just remember that the vessel is completely hard/stiff and you cannot bend or twist it at all.

2. Blockage of arteries.  **Add water**
   I associate it with the second stop that is 'add water'. To link both you can imagine a huge blood artery with a blockage; to remove you are adding water to wash it out.

3. Dying heart cell.  **Stove**
   This I can easily associate with the stove. Imagine that you have put the heart on the 'stove' and because of the heat of the stove, the heart's cells are dying. To make it more vivid in your memory, see the heart cells crying out for help as they are dying.

4. Valve damage.  **Tea leaves**
   The fourth stop in the journey is 'tea leaves'. Visualize

the valve of the heart and find out that the valve is not working as it damaged. To cure you are pasting some crushed tea leaves on it.

5. Diabetes. **Add sugar**
The fifth stop of the tea journey is 'sugar'. Coincidentally there is an automatic connection between sugar and diabetes. But here we must follow caution— my experience has shown that whenever there is an automatic correlation, we take it for granted and think that by default we will remember it. But in reality, when we need to recall the information, we get stuck and are unable to recall. You should not be tempted to opt for an automatic connection; instead you should create your own strong link. Here, you can imagine that a neighbour who is diabetic drops in to your house and demands tea with lots of sugar.

6. Abnormal heart rhythm. **Milk**
In our tea journey the sixth point is 'milk'. Imagine that a man is milking a cow to the rhythmic beat of drum; whenever the drumbeats stop the cow does not let the man go on milking.

7. High blood pressure. **Cup**
The seventh stop of the journey is 'cup'. Here again you can simply visualize any of your acquaintances who may be suffering from high blood pressure as sitting on top of the cup of tea.

Now the next time you need to recall the causes of heart failure, you just have to recall the process of making tea. And these stops will help you recall all the seven points.

Now take this small test to see if you can recall all the points or not. Fill in the blanks with the causes of heart failure:

...............................................

...............................................

...............................................

...............................................

...............................................

...............................................

...............................................

...............................................

### Create your own journey

Now, after two examples it is time for you to create your own journey. Think of a familiar setting—your school, university, office or nearby mall, and create a small journey of 10 stages. Later on when you are proficient in this method you can make longer journeys.

Create and revise mentally and write it here:

**Points to remember**

✓ Always choose a familiar setting to form journeys.
✓ Do not take much time to create a perfect journey.
✓ Make your journey a logical one—that is, choose to move clockwise or anti-clockwise.
✓ Practice the journey until you feel confident. It won't take much time.
✓ Make colourful, moving, interesting, even weird, associations with journey stages to memorize.

1. ......................................................
2. ......................................................
3. ......................................................
4. ......................................................
5. ......................................................
6. ......................................................
7. ......................................................
8. ......................................................
9. ......................................................
10. ....................................................

## Exercise

Now, try this to-do list with this newly formed journey. See vivid images in your mind, try to put humour and emotions in the associations and have some fun.

1. Depositing a cheque.
2. Going to an ATM for cash.
3. Getting the air-conditioner serviced.
4. Wishing a friend on his birthday.
5. Buying fruits and vegetables.
6. Writing an email to your boss.
7. Giving a coat for alteration to your tailor.
8. Formatting your spouse's computer.
9. Appointing a gardener.
10. Arranging clothes in your cupboard.

Revise once more and see how many of them you can remember.

| Journey stops | Work to do |
|---|---|
| | |
| | |
| | |
| | |
| | |
| | |
| | |
| | |
| | |
| | |

By now I hope you have achieved mastery in the use of the Journey Method. With your creative brain, you can create your own journey for different situations.

# CHAPTER 6

---

# NEVER FORGET A NUMBER

IN THIS world most of the things we need to memorize are defined by either words or numbers. These are the two that we usually try to memorize as an audio file and that is the reason why we are not able to store these memories for a long period. As I discussed earlier, audio files leak from what I call 'memory holes'.

So in this chapter you are going to learn an interesting technique called the **Number Method** and through this technique you can tackle any kind of numbers.

There are many events in our life where we realize that we are not able to recollect so many things and most of them are numbers. For example, someone's house number, mobile number, credit card PIN, ATM PIN, bank locker number, birthdays, anniversaries, melting point, boiling point, historical dates, some physical constants, geographical coordinates, statistics, or some business numerical data.

These all are numbers and numbers are audio files; this is why you fail to remember them.

For example, if I tell you that my mobile number is 9312286540 and ask you to close the book and recall this number, I know that if you are among 99 per cent of the population of the world, you will not be able to recall even a part of the number. It does not mean that you have a poor memory or that your brain is unable to handle the numbers, it just means that numbers are abstract, numbers are meaningless, and numbers are simply audio files. Your brain can hold only up to five digits and a mobile number is double that size. If you read a five-digit telephone number, for example 24819, and close the book and try to recall it, and if you are among 99 per cent of the population, then you will be able to recall it correctly this time, because your brain can hold numbers up to five digits. But again this does not mean that it will become a permanent memory. You will be able to hold it for few minutes only. And later even this five-digit number will vanish from recall, because after all this is an audio file. Your brain does not hold an audio file even if it is very small or looks very simple.

Now the question is how do we convert numbers into a video file? For that you are going to come across an interesting technique called the Number Method.

By using this technique you can learn any number in the world and once you use this technique not only can you learn numbers very quickly but also retain them almost permanently, provided you use this technique properly.

## Learning the Number Method

In this method we assign letters or sounds to all the digits from 0 to 9.

For example, 1 is assigned the letters t and d. The tip to remember is that both t & d have a single downward stroke like that of 1.

| Digit | Letters | Tip to remember |
|-------|---------|-----------------|
| 0 | *S* | O is round and 'S' for sun is also round |
| 1 | *td* | both t and d have a single downward stroke |
| 2 | *n* | both n and 2 have two downward strokes |
| 3 | *m* | both 3 and m have three downward strokes |
| 4 | *X* | in all languages of the world 4 always ends in r |
| 5 | *L* | if we hold up the five fingers of the hand they take the shape of L |
| 6 | *G J* | G looks like 6, J is the mirror image of 6 |
| 7 | *K* | if we join two 7s they make a k |

| 8 | | f in cursive hand resembles 8, see shadow of v in water it looks like 8 |
|---|---|---|
| 9 | | both the letters resemble 9 |

Here, in this chapter, you will find a number of tests to practise. Only then will you be able to efficiently use the Number Method.

To understand further, go through the Exercise 1.

## Exercise 1

Once this is completed you are now ready to take the test, after getting the required percentage, you can make your way to the next stage of memory development.

Try to answer the following questions in three minutes:

1. In Phonetics, j stands for:
   a) 7          b) 4          c) 9          d) 6
2. In Phonetics, p stands for:
   a) 9          b) 6          c) 2          d) 3
3. In Phonetics, 0 stands for:
   a) I          b) g          c) s          d) L
4. In Phonetics, 8 stands for:
   a) p, b       b) f, v       c) k, j       d) s, d
5. In Phonetics, m stands for:
   a) 7          b) 4          c) 3          d) 9
6. In Phonetics, L stands for:
   a) 5          b) 3          c) 9          d) 4

7. In Phonetics, 6 stands for:
   a) t and l      b) f and v      c) m and d      d) g and j
8. In Phonetics, t stands for:
   a) 5            b) 1            c) 7            d) 9
9. In Phonetics, 9 stands for:
   a) d, b         b) p, b         c) l, g         d) s, t

Unlike other chapters, you are going to attempt many tests here because this method requires practice. Only then will you have a good hold on the Number Method and it will help you in the future. But now with the above test, you might have a complete hold on each of the letters for the various digits from 0 to 9.

### How to connect a number to an image using this method:

It is very simple to attach an image to a number using the Number Method.

For example if I say that your friend's house number is 47. Your memory may confuse you by recalling it as being either 47 or 74, but with the Number Method you simply recall it like this:

4 stands for 'r', and 7 for 'k'. Can you think of any word having r and k? Ok, it can be rack or rock. I find rock more interesting so I choose rock. Just imagine that when you enter the house of your friend (house number 47) you find it full of rocks. Instead of sitting on a sofa you are sitting on a rock. Your friend is lying on a rock instead of a bed.

So next time you need to recall his house number, visualize what he is doing at home and you will recall your friend lying on a rock. Convert this into a number i.e. r is 4, o is nothing and c is nothing and k is 7, automatically it will become 47. You can do this with ease only when you have had enough practice.

Let us do some more tests to gain expertise in this method. While creating the words remember, the exact spellings do not matter, just the sound of the word, which you chose because of the letters that matched your number. Like I chose 'rock' because of 'r' for 4 and 'k' for 7.

## Exercise 2

Try to answer the following questions in three minutes:

1.  In Phonetics, RaJa stands for:
    a) 72          b) 91          c) 46          d) 05

2.  In Phonetics, KaLia stands for:
    a) 25          b) 75          c) 15          d) 95

3.  In Phonetics, 58 stands for:
    a) LeaF        b) BaG         c) JasSi       d) BeLl

4.  In Phonetics, 84 stands for:
    a) PuB         b) FiLe        c) NaNa        d) FiRe

5.  In Phonetics, PM stands for:
    a) 72          b) 37          c) 49          d) 93

6.  In Phonetics, LaB stands for:
    a) 15          b) 27          c) 94          d) 59

7.  In Phonetics, 61 stands for:
    a) GirL        b) JeT         c) MaT         d) FeeT

8.  In Phonetics, JeaN stands for:
    a) 62          b) 52          c) 68          d) 41

9.  In Phonetics, 39 stands for:
    a) JaR         b) SeaT        c) MaP         d) LoG

10. In Phonetics, JaSsi stands for:
    a) 20          b) 40          c) 80          d) 60

11. In Phonetics, LaSe stands for:
    a) 70          b) 50          c) 30          d) 90

12. In Phonetics, FaN stands for:
    a) 39          b) 58          c) 83          d) 82

13. In Phonetics, MiKe stands for:
    a) 27          b) 64          c) 81          d) 37

14. In Phonetics, 52 stands for:
    a) JaiL        b) GoaT        c) DoG         d) LioN

15. In Phonetics, MooN stands for:
    a) 96          b) 67          c) 02          d) 32

16. In Phonetics, 15 stands for:
    a) DoLl        b) LoTa        c) Tie        d) GoD
17. In Phonetics, NaaG stands for:
    a) 69          b) 26          c) 47         d) 06
18. In Phonetics 71 stands for:
    a) LioN        b) TiGeR       c) KaP        d) KaT
19. In Phonetics, 92 stands for:
    a) RiN         b) TiM         c) BiN        d) ViM
20. In Phonetics, 27 stands for:
    a) NecK        b) LeG         c) HanD       d) HeaD
21. In Phonetics, 80 stands for:
    a) FuSe        b) RuSe        c) DoSe       d) GooSe
22. In Phonetics, 86 stands for:
    a) FauJi       b) LoTa        c) ViM        d) SocK
23. In Phonetics, SiM stands for:
    a) 68          b) 15          c) 03         d) 04
24. In Phonetics, 67 stands for:
    a) TaG         b) JacKy       c) DJ         d) LocK
25. In Phonetics, BaR stands for:
    a) 37          b) 93          c) 54         d) 94
26. In Phonetics, GF stands for:
    a) 68          b) 96          c) 56         d) 87
27. In Phonetics, 97 stands for:
    a) Tie         b) LifT        c) GifT       d) BiKe
28. In Phonetics, 01 stands for:
    a) StaR        b) SuiT        c) StaLl      d) SteaL
29. In Phonetics, 58 stands for:
    a) LaKe        b) GoD         c) DeaD       d) LeaF
30. In Phonetics, 64 stands for:
    a) TeaM        b) JaR         c) LoTa       d) KaT

31. In Phonetics, MuG stands for:
   a) 37       b) 34       c) 36       d) 39

32. In Phonetics, L.G. stands for:
   a) 56       b) 59       c) 53       d) 57

33. In Phonetics, LioN stands for:
   a) 94       b) 14       c) 74       d) 52

34. In Phonetics, SiR stands for:
   a) 04       b) 10       c) 28       d) 60

35. In Phonetics, 71 stands for:
   a) ToY       b) LaP       c) None       d) Dice

36. In Phonetics, BaT stands for:
   a) 71       b) 1 6       c) 91       d) 52

37. In Phonetics, ReaR stands for:
   a) 68       b) 23       c) 44       d) 56

38. In Phonetics, DoSa stands for:
   a) 10       b) 90       c) 40       d) 70

39. In Phonetics, AmiR stands for:
   a) 37       b) 46       c) 34       d) 39

40. In Phonetics, FP stands for:
   a) 58       b) 35       c) 91       d) 89

**Answers:**

40.FP-89
33.Lion-52 34.Sir-04 35.71-none of them 36.Bat-91 37.Rear-44 38.Dosa-10 39.Amir-34
Bar-94 26.GF-68 27. 97-bike 28. 01-suit 29.58-leaf 30.64-jar 31.Mug-36 32. LG-56
26 18.71-kat 19.92-bin 20.27-neck 21.80-fuse 22.86-fauji 23.Sim-04 24.67-jacky 25.
10.Jassi-60 11.Lase-50 12.Fan-82 13.Mike-37 14.Moon-32 15.15-Doli 16.Naag-26 17.Naag-
1.Raja-46 2.Kalia-75 3.58-Leaf 4.84-File 5.PM-93 6.Lab-59 7.61-jet 8.Jean-62 9.39-map

As I mentioned earlier, in this chapter you will find a number of tests (unlike other chapters) because this method is based on exercises. If you practise properly, you can apply it with ease, or else it will feel like a burden.

Now, it is time to try out this method.

## Historical dates

You can use this method to memorize historical dates. This means you need to convert the historical dates into an equivalent picture using this method and then associate it with the event. Ignore the first number-'1'-as it is the first digit of almost every well-known year. This is my way to learn historical dates, but you can formulate your own styles of remembering.

### 1707: Death of Aurangzeb

(1)-7-0-7 Aurangzeb death

Think of the words that contain K(7)-S(0)-K(7); it may be 'kiosk'. You can visualize that Aurangzeb died and his body is kept inside the kiosk rather than buried in a cemetery.

## 1889: Birth of Pandit Nehru

(1)-8-8-9 Pandit Nehru born

Think of a word with letters V(8)-V(8)-P(9), to my mind comes the word 'VVIP'. Of course Pandit Nehru was a VVIP as he was the first prime minister of our country. Visualize that baby Pandit Nehru was placed in a VIP suitcase when he was born and this made him very, very important from the very beginning.

## 1927: American aviator Charles Lindbergh made the first flight across the Atlantic Ocean

(1)-9-2-7 Lindbergh

P(9)-N(2)-K(7), suggests a picture 'pink'. Visualize Lindbergh flying over the Atlantic Ocean in a PiNk aeroplane.

### 1914: First World War

(1)-9-1-4 First World War

B(9)-T(1)-R(4), these letters propose to me the word 'BaTTeRy'. You can connect it to the event by thinking that in the First World War, guns were battery-operated as technology was not that advanced at the time. (TT is considered a single letter as you only hear the single sound of T).

### 1942: Quit India Movement
(1)-9-4-2 Quit India Movement

Think of the words with letters B(9)-R(4)-N(2). What about BRaiN? Think—Mahatma Gandhi launched the Quit India Movement for freedom from British rule using his brain.

### 1933: Adolf Hitler appointed Chancellor of Germany
B(9)-M(3)-M(3) any suitable word containing these letters. No such word is clicking to my mind. In such cases you can split the number into two parts (9 and 33). As a rule, you can use Shape Method in the first part and Number Method for the second part.

The number 9 looks like a lollipop as per the shape method, and 33 is MaMa. Now, you can imagine that Hitler has become Chancellor of Germany and his MaMa (33, Mother) is giving him a lollipop (9).

## Exercise 3

Now, try these dates yourself.

### 1. 1912: Invention of the parachute

B (9)-T (1)-N (2) is BuTtoN
Button (912)—Parachutes invented
Imaginary Link:

..............................................................................................

..............................................................................................

..............................................................................................

## 2. 1920: First commercial radio broadcast aired

(P)9-(N)2-(S)0 is PiNS

Pins (920)—First Commercial Radio Broadcast

Imaginary Link:

......................................................................................................

......................................................................................................

......................................................................................................

## 3. 1924: First Olympic Winter Games

B(9)-N(2)-R(4) is BaNneR

Banner (924)—First Olympic Winter Games

Imaginary Link:

......................................................................................................

......................................................................................................

......................................................................................................

## 4. 1930: Gandhi's Salt March

B(9)-M(3)-S(0) is BeaMS

Beams—Gandhi's Salt March

Imaginary Link:

......................................................................................................

......................................................................................................

......................................................................................................

## 5. 1939: World's first helicopter is made

B(9)-M(3)-P(9) is BuMP

Bump—Helicopter Invented

Imaginary Link:

......................................................................................................

......................................................................................................

......................................................................................................

You might have got some ideas on how to tackle history dates using this method. Now it's time to try your own list of history dates in this manner.

## Learn the Periodic Table

I know if are you among other average readers you may be tempted to skip these tests and go directly to the next paragraph or next example. But please try to understand that these tests are equally important, because they will become a building block to understand further examples. So if you are among those who have skipped the tests, please go back and work through them sincerely, even if it takes some time.

Now that you have done all the tests and are confident, we can use the same method to memorize the Periodic Table. Let's say you want to memorize the atomic number of tungsten, which is 74. Now you know after some time you may confuse 74 with 47, as both are audio files. So you need to use the Number Method to convert this. You know 7 is 'k' and 4 is 'r' you may visualize a KaR (car) for 74 (ignore the spelling, it does not matter). Now you need to attach a video file with tungsten using the Word Image System (WIS), and the closest word I can think of is 'tongue'. So, the word 'tongue' is enough to recall the actual element tungsten.

I can associate a boy is cleaning a car (74) with his tongue (tungsten). This ridiculous picture will help to remember the atomic number of tungsten for a long period.

Similarly, you can apply the Number Method to the Periodic Table to remember the audio files of atomic numbers, and use WIS to remember the name of the elements.

### Exercise 4

Please try to link the image of the element with that of the number in the test below:

| Elements | At. Number | Element Image | At. Image |
|---|---|---|---|
| Hydrogen (H) | 01 | Hydrogen balloon | SuiT |
| Link...................................................................................................... | | | |
| .................................................................................................................. | | | |

| Elements | At. Number | Element Image | At. Image |
|---|---|---|---|
| Helium (He) | 02 | Helen (Actor) | SuN |
| Link...................................................................................................... | | | |
| .................................................................................................................. | | | |

| Elements | At. Number | Element Image | At. Image |
|---|---|---|---|
| Lithium (Li) | 03 | Litchi | SiM (card) |
| Link...................................................................................................... | | | |

| Elements | At. Number | Element Image | At. Image |
|---|---|---|---|
| Beryllium (Be) | 04 | Berry | SiR (Teacher) |

Link.....................................................................................................

| Elements | At. Number | Element Image | At. Image |
|---|---|---|---|
| Carbon (C) | 06 | Car and bun | SaGe |

Link.....................................................................................................

| Elements | At. Number | Element Image | At. Image |
|---|---|---|---|
| Nitrogen (N) | 07 | Night | SKy |

Link.....................................................................................................

| Elements | At. Number | Element Image | At. Image |
|---|---|---|---|
| Oxygen (O) | 08 | Ox | SoFa |

Link.....................................................................................................

| Elements | At. Number | Element Image | At. Image |
|---|---|---|---|
| Fluorine (F) | 09 | Floor and rin | SoaP |

Link.....................................................................................................

| Elements | At. Number | Element Image | At. Image |
|---|---|---|---|
| Neon (Ne) | 10 | Knee | DoSa |

Link.....................................................................................................

| Elements | At. Number | Element Image | At. Image |
|---|---|---|---|
| Magnesium (Mg) | 12 | Mango | DeN |

Link...................................................................................................

.......................................................................................................

| Elements | At. Number | Element Image At. | Image |
|----------|-----------|-------------------|-------|
| Silicon (Si) | 14 | Cell and cone | DaRa (Singh) |

Link...................................................................................................

.......................................................................................................

| Elements | At. Number | Element Image At. | Image |
|----------|-----------|-------------------|-------|
| Phosphorus (P) | 15 | Fox | DolL |

Link...................................................................................................

.......................................................................................................

| Elements | At. Number | Element Image At. | Image |
|----------|-----------|-------------------|-------|
| Sulphur (S) | 16 | Cell and fur | DoG |

Link...................................................................................................

.......................................................................................................

| Elements | At. Number | Element Image At. | Image |
|----------|-----------|-------------------|-------|
| Chlorine (Cl) | 17 | Clown | DecK (Music) |

Link...................................................................................................

.......................................................................................................

| Elements | At. Number | Element Image At. | Image |
|----------|-----------|-------------------|-------|
| Argon (Ar) | 18 | Air gun | ToFfee |

Link...................................................................................................

.......................................................................................................

| Elements | At. Number | Element Image At. | Image |
|----------|-----------|-------------------|-------|
| Potassium (K) | 19 | Pot | TaP |

Link...................................................................................................

.......................................................................................................

| Elements | At. Number | Element Image | At. | Image |
|---|---|---|---|---|
| Calcium (Ca) | 20 | CalciumSandoztablet | | NoSe |
| Link.................................................................................................
................................................................................ | | | | |

| Elements | At. Number | Element Image | At. | Image |
|---|---|---|---|---|
| Scandium (Sc) | 21 | Scan | | NeT |
| Link.................................................................................................
................................................................................ | | | | |

| Elements | At. Number | Element Image | At. | Image |
|---|---|---|---|---|
| Titanium (Ti) | 22 | Titanic (ship) | | NaNa |
| Link.................................................................................................
................................................................................ | | | | |

| Elements | At. Number | Element Image | At. | Image |
|---|---|---|---|---|
| Vanadium (V) | 23 | Van (Any school van) | | NeeM |
| Link.................................................................................................
................................................................................ | | | | |

| Elements | At. Number | Element Image | At. | Image |
|---|---|---|---|---|
| Cobalt (Co) | 27 | Cobbler | | NecK |
| Link.................................................................................................
................................................................................ | | | | |

| Elements | At. Number | Element Image | At. | Image |
|---|---|---|---|---|
| Copper (Cu) | 29 | Cop | | NiB |
| Link.................................................................................................
................................................................................ | | | | |

| Elements | At. Number | Element Image | At. | Image |
|---|---|---|---|---|
| Germanium (Ge) | 32 | German (language) | | MooN |
| Link.................................................................................................
................................................................................ | | | | |

| Elements | At. Number | Element Image At. | Image |
|---|---|---|---|
| Selenium (Se) | 34 | Celina (Jaitley, actor) | aMiR (Khan, actor) |
| Link............................................................................................ |||
| ............................................................................................ |||

| Elements | At. Number | Element Image At. | Image |
|---|---|---|---|
| Bromine (Br) | 35 | Broom | MaiL |
| Link............................................................................................ |||
| ............................................................................................ |||

| Elements | At. Number | Element Image At. | Image |
|---|---|---|---|
| Strontium (Sr) | 38 | Straw (pipe) | MF (Hussain painter) |
| Link............................................................................................ |||
| ............................................................................................ |||

| Elements | At. Number | Element Image At. | Image |
|---|---|---|---|
| Niobium (Nb) | 41 | New bomb | RaT |
| Link............................................................................................ |||
| ............................................................................................ |||

| Elements | At. Number | Element Image At. | Image |
|---|---|---|---|
| Rhodium (Rh) | 45 | Road | RaiL |
| Link............................................................................................ |||
| ............................................................................................ |||

| Elements | At. Number | Element Image At. | Image |
|---|---|---|---|
| Silver (Ag) | 47 | Silver | RacK |
| Link............................................................................................ |||
| ............................................................................................ |||

| Elements | At. Number | Element Image At. | Image |
|---|---|---|---|
| Cadmium (Cd) | 48 | Cadbury (chocolate) | RooF |

Link........................................................................................................
................................................................................................................

| Elements | At. Number | Element Image At. | Image |
|---|---|---|---|
| Indium (In) | 49 | Indian | RoPe |

Link........................................................................................................
................................................................................................................

| Elements | At. Number | Element Image At. | Image |
|---|---|---|---|
| Tin (Sn) | 50 | Tin | LaSe (Lace) |

Link........................................................................................................
................................................................................................................

| Elements | At. Number | Element Image At. | Image |
|---|---|---|---|
| Tellurium (Te) | 52 | Talcum powder | LioN |

Link........................................................................................................
................................................................................................................

| Elements | At. Number | Element Image At. | Image |
|---|---|---|---|
| Iodine (I) | 53 | Iodex | LiMe |

Link........................................................................................................
................................................................................................................

| Elements | At. Number | Element Image At. | Image |
|---|---|---|---|
| Barium (Ba) | 56 | Bar (soap) | LG (TV) |

Link........................................................................................................
................................................................................................................

| Elements | At. Number | Element Image At. | Image |
|---|---|---|---|
| Lanthanum (La) | 57 | Lantern | LaKe |

Link........................................................................................................

| Elements | At. Number | Element Image At. | Image |
|---|---|---|---|
| Cerium (Ce) | 58 | Cereals | LeaF |
| Link........................................................................................................ | | | |
| ............................................................................................................... | | | |

| Elements | At. Number | Element Image At. | Image |
|---|---|---|---|
| Praseodymium (Pr) | 59 | President | LaB |
| Link........................................................................................................ | | | |
| ............................................................................................................... | | | |

| Elements | At. Number | Element Image At. | Image |
|---|---|---|---|
| Samarium (Sm) | 62 | Samurai | JeaNs |
| Link........................................................................................................ | | | |
| ............................................................................................................... | | | |

| Elements | At. Number | Element Image At. | Image |
|---|---|---|---|
| Europium (Eu) | 63 | Europe | JaM |
| Link........................................................................................................ | | | |
| ............................................................................................................... | | | |

| Elements | At. Number | Element Image At. | Image |
|---|---|---|---|
| Terbium (Tb) | 65 | Turbun | JaiL |
| Link........................................................................................................ | | | |
| ............................................................................................................... | | | |

| Elements | At. Number | Element Image At. | Image |
|---|---|---|---|
| Dysprosium (Dy) | 66 | Dice | JuG |
| Link........................................................................................................ | | | |
| ............................................................................................................... | | | |

| Elements | At. Number | Element Image At. | Image |
|---|---|---|---|
| Holmium (Ho) | 67 | Hole | JacKy (Shroff, actor) |
| Link........................................................................................................ | | | |
| ............................................................................................................... | | | |

| Elements | At. Number | Element Image At. | Image |
|---|---|---|---|
| Erbium (Er) | 68 | Ear | GF (Girl friend) |

Link.................................................................................................
.................................................................................................

| Elements | At. Number | Element Image At. | Image |
|---|---|---|---|
| Gold (Au) | 79 | Gold | KaP (Cap) |

Link.................................................................................................
.................................................................................................

| Elements | At. Number | Element Image At. | Image |
|---|---|---|---|
| Mercury (Hg) | 80 | Mercury thermometer | FuSe |

Link.................................................................................................
.................................................................................................

| Elements | At. Number | Element Image At. | Image |
|---|---|---|---|
| Lead (Pb) | 82 | Lead (pencil) | FaN |

Link.................................................................................................
.................................................................................................

| Elements | At. Number | Element Image At. | Image |
|---|---|---|---|
| Bismuth (Bi) | 83 | Blacksmith | F.M. (Radio) |

Link.................................................................................................
.................................................................................................

| Elements | At. Number | Element Image At. | Image |
|---|---|---|---|
| Francium (Fr) | 87 | Fancy Dress | ForK |

Link.................................................................................................
.................................................................................................

| Elements | At. Number | Element Image | At. Image |
|---|---|---|---|
| Protactinium (Pa) | 91 | Protector | PoT (Flower) |
| Link............................................................................................... | | | |
| ............................................................................................... | | | |

| Elements | At. Number | Element Image | At. Image |
|---|---|---|---|
| Neptunium (Np) | 93 | Naphthalene ball | PM |
| Link............................................................................................... | | | |
| ............................................................................................... | | | |

| Elements | At. Number | Element Image | At. Image |
|---|---|---|---|
| Plutonium (Pu) | 94 | Pluto | BaR |
| Link............................................................................................... | | | |
| ............................................................................................... | | | |

| Elements | At. Number | Element Image | At. Image |
|---|---|---|---|
| Californium (Cf) | 98 | California | BF(Boy friend) |
| Link............................................................................................... | | | |
| ............................................................................................... | | | |

| Elements | At. Number | Element Image | At. Image |
|---|---|---|---|
| Einsteinium (Es) | 99 | Einstein | BaBy |
| Link............................................................................................... | | | |
| ............................................................................................... | | | |

| Elements | At. Number | Element Image | At. Image |
|---|---|---|---|
| Fermium (Fm) | 100 | Firm (company) | TheSiS |
| Link............................................................................................... | | | |
| ............................................................................................... | | | |

| Elements | At. Number | Element Image | At. Image |
|---|---|---|---|
| Mendelevium (Md) | 101 | Mandoline | TeST |

Link..........................................................................................................

..........................................................................................................

## More Examples

### Melting point of lead is 327 degrees Celsius

You know that 327 is an audio file so it is possible you may confuse it with 327 or 237. Simply remember it like this:

> 3 is m, 2 is n and 7 is k. So think of a word which contains all these three letters along with some vowels, and immediately your mind will say 'MoNKey'. Now monkey is a video file, easy to remember; whereas 327 is an audio file, much more difficult to remember. To remember that lead has a melting point of 327, convert 327 into an equivalent video file, i.e. monkey.

You can imagine that you are writing with a lead pencil and a monkey jumps in and snatches your lead pencil and runs away. So next time when your teacher asks you the melting point of lead, that very thought of a lead pencil will take you to the image of a monkey, and if you decode MoNKey you will know it is 327. This way you will remember without confusion that the melting point of lead is 327 degrees Celsius.

## Atomic mass of mercury is 201

Since 201 is an audio file, after sometime you may not be able to recollect it correctly. But with this method, to secure it to your memory is very simple—2 is N, 0 is S and 1 is T and it becomes NeST. So 'nest' is one picture your brain can easily remember whereas 201 is an audio file which your brain finds difficult to remember. This means there are numerous ways to connect the word 'mercury' with 'nest' i.e. 201.

But again mercury is an audio file, so convert it into a video file by thinking of some visual that can represent mercury. What kind of output does your brain give for the keyword 'mercury'? For me, mercury means Mercury the planet or mercury in a thermometer; I can choose any video file which may interest me. Let me chose mercury thermometer. I can visualize placing a mercury thermometer inside a nest to keep an eye on its temperature.

So the next time the teacher asks the atomic mass of mercury, the image of the mercury thermometer will bring to mind the video file of the nest. Decode the word NeST and it will be 201.

## Atomic mass of gold is 197

D(1)-P(9)-K(7)—DeePaK, you can imagine that your friend Deepak is wearing kilos of gold and sitting in the class. So next time when someone asks you the atomic mass unit of gold, you will remember Deepak, and DeePaK means 197.

### House number with block

You happen to meet your childhood friend, Rajesh Sharma, in the market after a long time. You come to know that he has finally settled here in your town. He insists you to visit his house and tells you that his house number is 357. You know that you will forget his house number by the time you reach home, so you immediately convert 3 (M)-5(L)-7(K) into the video file by thinking of 'MiLK'.

To establish a connection of his house number to your brain think like this—when you go to Rajesh's house, he opens the door and you see milk everywhere; in fact, he is swimming in the milk (357).

He further tells you that his block number is 'E'. I am sure you will not remember this either as it is a single letter and is meaningless. So go back to your childhood memory and ask of yourself:

A is for ......................**a**pple

B is for...................... **b**all

C is for...................... **c**at

D is for...................... **d**og

And

E is for......................**e**lephant, for most of us.

Now, to associate the block number think that Rajesh has drunk so much milk (357) that he has become fat and huge like an elephant (E).

## Memorizing Sections or a Subsection

### Section 147: Giving publishing rights

If you are reading a lot of sections then there is a good chance that you may get confused later as to whether it was 147 or 247. To register it your memory, simply think of an image of section 147—a TRucK (1 is T, 4 is R and 7 is K). This means you just need to associate the truck with the content with which you want to remember it, i.e. publishing rights.

Imagine your publisher has given all the rights of publication to you and you are loading all the books and documents of publishing rights on to a truck.

## Security PIN of an ATM Card

Suppose you need to remember that the ATM PIN of your ICICI bank card is 7463. First turn the number into letters:

### 7 4 6 3 is K R J M

Think of a word containing these letters that should be easy for you to remember. For example, you might think of,

KaRJaM

Visualize a car jam in front of your ATM and you are on the other side of the road, struggling to reach the ATM. Once more, keep in mind that accurate spellings do not matter.

With these examples you might have understood that converting a number into an image is a way to learn them permanently. So, in this way, you can handle any number— whether it is a number related to any syllabus or your day-to-day life.

I use the same strategy to remember the numbers of my use. When I hear the telephone number I simultaneously convert it into a picture using the Number Method. Once it is done it is almost secured in the mind lifelong. But you will be able to do this only when you practise and that is the reason why I set practice tests in this chapter. Only after the practice will you be able to appreciate this fantastic method. Otherwise at the first glance it may not appear to be very encouraging.

So for example if you want to remember an office number it is very easy if you convert this into a mental video:

2510534

Imagine a NaiL(25) which you are inserting into a DoSa(10). By the time you did it you realized that a LoMRi (534 Hindi word meaning fox) is coming running towards you. This mental picture is a sketch of the telephone number, i.e. 2510534. 2510534 is a meaningless audio file which you might not remember, but yes, the mental movie of this number will certainly help you recall the number.

My game plan, when I want to remember something for personal use, is to use all the languages I know—English, Hindi, Punjabi and sometimes even Bangla too. Using multiple languages makes me remember better. You may also use multiple languages as per your knowledge and preference.

I would like to emphasize again is that too you need intensive practice and patience for this method to work for you.

## CHAPTER 7

---

# FROM ROAD MAPS TO BIOLOGICAL DIAGRAMS

By NOW, you might have understood that there is no such thing as a good or bad memory, it is all about a trained or untrained memory. It is about making a list of situations where you would like your memory to work smartly and then using the memory formula to customise and create a method for a particular situation.

For example, let's take a hypothetical situation; here I am giving you the directions to my house.

From Nehru bus stop, go straight till you reach a flyover. From the flyover, take a left turn till you reach a police station and then take a right turn and reach the over-bridge. Then take a U-turn and now take a left turn from the third traffic light. Go straight till you hit a T-point. Take a right turn and reach a building called the 'World Tower'. Now take a left turn...

I am sure you must be thoroughly confused by now. Even so, try to answer some of my questions related to the directions:

1. After World Tower, turn ................
2. After police station, turn................
3. A T-point, turn................
4. From over-bridge, turn................

Here, if your memory works like most of the human species you might score nearly 25 per cent. But don't worry this is not an example of a bad memory. This is just an untrained memory. Now, let's try to investigate the answers of these two questions:

**1**: Why could you not memorize these directions?
**2**: How can you perfect your memory for road maps?

**Answer 1**: Clearly, what you failed to memorize here are 'directions'. You tried to recall whether it was a left or a right or a U-turn. The reason is simple:

## Video File >Memory Leakage Hole >Audio File

Since directions do not have any particular shape or colour, they come under the category of an audio file and you know that audio files leak out of our memory.

**Answer 2**: Now, you have two options to remember the road directions. Either you keep on repeating and revising every now and then in order to have a definite stock of audio files of directions. Or, we can train our memory and convert the directions into video files, and your trained memory will be able to handle all kind of directions without confusion lifelong.

Read the list below aloud:

Left-Leaf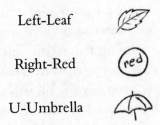

Right-Red

U-Umbrella

You have given a video file to each of the three symbols, i.e. for left, imagine a leaf, for right turn, think of red and for U-turn, visualize an umbrella. The first letter of each of the word will help you remember the representative video file. Next time you want to remember a direction just visualize leaf for left turn and so on. You will find it amazingly easy to remember road maps and directions. Let's give it a try. Think of this new route:

Go straight from the bus stand till you reach the **Clock Tower** and then take a left turn (imagine a leafy clock tower), keep moving till you reach the **cloth shop** then take a right (imagine the shop full of red clothes). Next take a

U-turn from the **furniture market** (imagine an umbrella on all the furniture). Now, take a left turn from the **book shop** (imagine books with leaves in it). Turn right from the **Maruti car showroom** (here imagine all red cars). After walking some distance you will find a **Hanuman Temple,** take a U-turn (visualize Hanumanji holding an umbrella). Now, keep moving till you get to **Sagar Ratna Restaurant** and take a left turn (imagine all the waiters wearing leaves or serving leaves). Take a right turn from the **post office** (a red coloured post office). Now, turn right from the **chicken shop** (bleeding red chicken). Now, move left from the **tuition centre board** (imagine a big leaf on the board) and finally take a U-turn from a small **pond** (pond full of umbrellas) and you will reach the destination.

Now, before you judge whether or not you have memorized the road map perfectly, let's take a test:

1. You have to take a.............turn from the clock tower.
   (Cue: Think all the three video files for the respective turns and automatically the right answer will pop up).
2. .............turn from the book shop.
3. Take.............turn from Hanuman temple.
4. You need to take .......turn from the furniture shop.
5. Take ...............from the Maruti showroom.
6. What was the turn from Sagar Ratna Restaurant?.............
7. Turn from chicken shop was.............
8. Which turn from tuition centre board?.....................
9. .............from the pond.
10. What was the turn from the post office?.............

## Remember the road map with a sequence of landmarks

If you are enjoying reading this book, then you may be among those who have scored more than 80 per cent in the tests till now. Now, the question may be what if you need to recall not only the directions with respect to the landmark but also the sequence of the landmarks in the required order.

Here, you might wonder why we are not using the Shape Method memory tool we discussed earlier. The reason we are not using it is that we do not need to have very long-term recall for items recalled with the Shape Method, such as shopping lists or appointments. But a long-term memory is required in the case of roadmaps so here the Journey Method proves more reliable.

Let's try using the journey of the drawing room of your home.

Position yourself at the door, the first stop of the journey as you prepare yourself to learn the roadmaps while reading or listening to it. As you hear the first landmark the clock tower, just imagine a leafy clock tower on the door and for the next landmark the cloth shop, connect it with the next stop of the journey, i.e. the sofa, in this case. Imagine a miniature cloth shop kept on the sofa. Similarly, try to link and visualize all the landmarks in the respective order with the respective stops of your journey. Use your creativity to embellish the associations. It is very important to embellish the associations to make them stick in the mind.

| Journey stop | Landmark | Cue |
|---|---|---|
| Door | Leafy Clock Tower | A leafy clock tower on the door |
| Sofa | Red Cloth Shop | A red cloth shop on the sofa |
| TV | Furniture Market | Furniture market with umbrella live show on TV |
| Curtains | Book Shop | Books with leaves hanging on curtains in a book shop |
| Table | Maruti Car Showroom | Maruti cars in red colour on the table |
| Painting | Hanuman Temple | Hanumanji with umbrella in painting |
| Table lamp | Sagar Ratna Restaurant | Sagar Ratna restaurant waiters wearing leaves under the table lamp |

| Computer | Post Office | Red coloured post office shown in computer |
|---|---|---|
| Carpet | Chicken Shop | Bleeding (red) chicken lying on the carpet |
| Window | Tuition-centre Board | Tuition-centre board with leaves on the window |
| Armchair | Pond | Armchair floating in a pond with umbrellas |

Considering that it is the first time you are attempting to learn a roadmap using the Journey Method do not worry if it takes little longer than ten minutes to do so, but ensure that you vividly associate and visualize each of the turns and landmarks with the respective journey stop. With some practice and application in real life you will be able to reduce the learning time to less than a minute for a similar length of roadmap route.

Now, test your trained memory once more:

1. The landmark after the Hanuman temple is..................
2. The landmark before the book shop is....................
3. The landmark before the clock tower is...................
4. The landmark following the cloth shop is...................
5. After the furniture market is...................
6. The Maruti showroom comes after...................
7. The landmark after Sagar Ratna restaurant is...................
8. The next landmark after the Post Office is...................
9. The landmark before the chicken shop is...................
10. The third landmark from the pond is...................
11. The landmark after the tuition-centre board is...................

I am sure you must have passed this test with flying colours. Before we move on to a different memory situation, I would like to give you a tip. Chose a partner and ask her/him to make an imaginary road map and read it out slowly. While listening, try to memorize the directions, using the technique you have just learned. This practice will not only build faith in the method, but will also give you many clues which will help you to manage various other kinds of memory situations.

## Biological Diagrams

Now, let's take another situation where you need to remember biological diagrams. Although, you may find this case to be entirely different from the previous one which we just concluded, the approach to train the memory to handle the biological diagrams is amazingly similar to the previous situation.

Two important questions here:

1. Why is it difficult to remember the biological diagrams?
2. How should we train the memory to act infallibly in handling various biological diagrams?

**Answer 1**: Look at these biological diagrams, among all the diagrams concentrate on the shape of the cuboidal cell. You will never forget it, since the name itself is the clue for the shape. Similarly, focus on the shape of the columnar cell, again its name reminds you of its shape; it is like a tall column. But unlike these two among the rest of the cells there is no automatic association and furthermore the names come under the category of 'audio files'. Now, once again have a look at the memory formula.

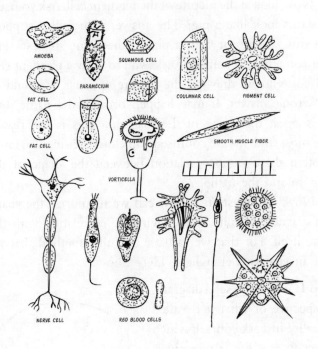

### Video File >Memory Leakage Hole >Audio File

Now, as you know, the names being audio files eventually leak out of our memory. Similarly, the random meaningless shapes of the cells also do not fit appropriately in the definition of the video files so they may also not stay in the memory.

**Answer 2**: By assigning images to all the three symbols of the road map, you produced an alternative video file.

Similarly, a glimpse of each of the cell diagrams will give you a clue of some specific video file.

Now, look at the picture of the pigment cell. Ask yourself, does this look like a pig? The answer is 'no'. But suppose you still associate it with a pig, as the name suggests, and after some time if someone asks you to draw a pigment cell, and you end up drawing the picture of a pig, it would be the wrong answer. It may happen because the name does not suggest the shape of the diagram. This is the reason why most students are confused while memorising diagrams, as often there is no corelation between the shape of the diagram and the name.

Now, the question is how can we memorize the shape of a diagram in spite of its having no correlation with the name itself. For that we can use a similar method that we have in fact used elsewhere. Here's how:

**Step 1**: When you see a diagram, irrespective of what it is called in reality, just ask yourself which object in real life it resembles. For instance, take the shape of the fat cell.

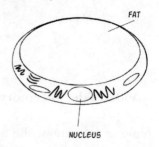

Have a close look at the fat cell and try to relate it with a real life object. It reminds me of a wedding ring. So, wedding ring cell would have been a better name for this cell as it would have made it easier for us to memorize.

Now, look at the shape of a paramecium cell. The very first glance gives you a hint that it looks like a slipper or a shoe. So, it would have been better if it was named as 'shoe or slipper cell'. But scientists named it 'paramecium'.

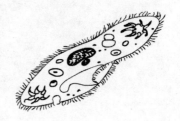

Similarly, take the 'olfactory cell', which, to many students, looks like a rat at the first glance. So, had it been called 'rat cell' we could have kept the shape in mind very easily.

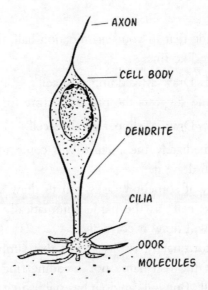

Look at another picture—the 'vorticella cell', which suggests to us the shape of a wine glass. So had it been called a 'wine glass cell', you would have learnt it better.

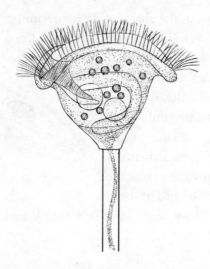

Now, imagine that in your examination hall, the test paper is something like this:

**Question 1**: Draw a 'wedding ring cell'.

The name suggests the precise picture for it.

**Question 2**: Draw a 'slipper or shoe cell'

So, immediately the picture will come to your mind and you will draw it.

Similarly, if somebody asks you to draw a 'rat cell' or a 'wine glass cell', as the name automatically suggests the shape, you will draw it correctly.

But unfortunately, reality is not that simple. And you have to give the real name not 'wedding ring cell' for the name 'fat cell'. But you can do it by establishing a connection between 'wedding ring' and a 'fat cell'. I do it easily by imagining that I am getting married to a 'fat man'. But the ring does not fit his finger so the marriage is cancelled.

The next example is one that you thought as 'shoe cell' but its real name is paramecium. It means you need to associate the name paramecium with shoe cell. You can do it by using the Word Image System (WIS) for the word paramecium. To me, paramecium sounds like 'Paragon shoe'. Paragon is a footwear company, as you might know.

Now, olfactory cell reminds me of an oil factory. Just imagine that an oil factory is infested with rats. So, olfactory will remind you of rat.

Now, consider the vorticella cell that looks like a 'wine glass'. But, how do you remember that vorticella cell looks like a wine glass? As you understand, vorticella is an audio file so first, you need to convert it to a video file. Again, you can do this by using WIS. Using this method:

Vorticella

War-T-sell (War-tea-sell)

During a war someone is selling tea

So, imagine that tea is being sold in a wine glass during a war.

This will help you to connect the audio file vorticella with the picture, i.e. the video of a wine glass.

Now, if your teacher asks you to draw the picture of a fat cell, the fat will help you to recollect the wedding ring and the picture of the wedding ring will remind you of the fat cell.

If you are asked to draw the picture of olfactory cell the audio word olfactory will lead you to the picture oil factory and then rats. And the shape of rats will help to remind you of the shape of the olfactory cell.

Similarly, for the pigment cell look at the word 'pig' and imagine the image of a pig. Have a look at the shape of the pigment cell—it looks like an octopus. Now, I can easily associate it with a ridiculous video that you put your hand in the mouth of a pig and what you take out is an octopus. Again I must add, these images are my imagination and aid my recall. Feel free to create other pictorial associations if these leave you scratching your head.

## Strategy Summary

You would have understood so far that shape, which at first glance looks like nothing familiar, can give you the hint of some daily-life object when you take a close look. And that gives you the clue for converting the shape of the diagram into a video file. Similarly you have to convert the name of a diagram into the video file using the Word Image System (WIS) and finally you need to connect it with video of the shape.

So the strategy remains the same, only content changes.

## Mathematical Formulae

By now, you might have understood two entirely dissimilar memory situations. But the approach to train your memory can still be similar. Let's try to solve some more memory problems with the same approach. Take the case of mathematical formulae. Among many students, the most common and basic confusion is to remember whether it was + or - , same as in the case of roadmap directions. As you know that + and - are symbols and they come under the category of audio files and so will always leak out of the memory hole, as a result you have to revise them every now and then. To remove the confusion easily and retain them forever, follow these rules.

## Convert the symbols to video files

| Audio | Video |
|:-----:|-------|
| + | Ambulance |
| - | Think of a negative character of reel/real life—maybe Osama Bin Laden or Dawood Ibrahim or even Gabbar Singh from the movie *Sholay*. |

Now, next time when you find the above symbol to be confusing to remember, then place these attentive equivalent video files in the formula and the correct formula will stick to your memory longer.

Similarly, you have to identify and make a list of other symbols and give them an alternative video file shape. Let's take an instance from trigonometry. In trigonometry there may be thousands of formulae but symbols are just six—

Sin
Cos
Tan
Cot
Sec
Cosec

All you have to do is to give each of them a suitable name which you may easily remember. I am sharing my personal choice of video files for your reference.

| Audio | Video |
|-------|-------|
| Sin | Cine (star) |
| Cos | Cosmetic |
| Tan | Tank |
| Cot | Cottage |
| Sec | Secretary |
| Cosec | Cassette |

Here, your choice of video files will matter a lot. Someone may conventionally think of 'sign' for Sin but try to understand that even though sin may be meaningful, it does not have a clear-cut interesting video file. Once you decide on an alternate shape/name for each of the symbols, it will remain a permanent identity for that symbol. And every time you memorize any formula featuring those symbols, you just have to replace it with a more memorable pre-decided video file. Let's take an example to understand exactly how it will work in this case. Take a look at some trigonometry formulae. The first one is:

$$\frac{d(\sin x)}{dx} = \cos x$$

Being a student of mathematics, you know that you need not memorize or use any techniques to remember d/dx= or the basic format of the formula; that you will remember as you have the understanding of the subject.

So, make rules to learn the formula.

## Step 1: Identify the problem

Find out what may be confusing to you. For example, take these six formulas—what is not confusing is d/dx = and the brackets, which you automatically remember. What is confusing is that in the first formula **sin x = cos x** whereas in the second formula **cos x = sin x**. So many times we are confused as to where a + is put and where a -; where a square root; a cube root; or an under root. Most of the time it happens because the symbols, as you know, are audio files. This simply means that you have to identify the point at which you begin get confused.

## Step 2: Fix it

All you have to do is to convert that confusion into a video file. How can you do that? Let's take the first example:

**sin x = cos x**

Imagination: Now, you go back to the memory and ask what sin x was. Sin x meant cine star so I can visualize my favourite cine star, say Hrithik Roshan. For cos x my picture is cosmetics, so I can imagine that my favourite cine star applying cosmetics on himself. That is all. But just thinking of the word cine star will not help you to visualize the picture of him. So to make it more memorable and impressive, I will further visualize Hrithik Roshan (cine star) applying cosmetics i.e. foundation, lipstick, etc. It might look ridiculous but it is the key for focusing and retaining.

Now, go to the next formula:

**cos x = sin x**

Here, the most important thing is that we must not confuse

whether it is minus or plus before sin x. That is why, you need to put more emphasis on the minus and now you know that 'minus' may not be remembered being an audio file. You have a corresponding video file for 'minus' and that is a 'villain'. In my case, my favourite villain is Gabbar Singh from *Sholay*. This means while imagining this formula, I have to imagine Gabbar Singh. How?

$$\cos x = \text{cosmetics}$$
$$- = \text{Gabbar Singh}$$
$$\sin x = \text{Cine star (Hrithik Roshan)}$$

Imagine Gabbar Singh applying cosmetics on Hrithik Roshan. It is not important whether the story is logical or not; what is important is the existence of a mental video. If you are successful in making a video file, then rest assured you will never forget it.

Similarly, consider the next example.

**Tan x = Sec$^2$x**

'Tan' is 'tank', and 'Sec' is 'secretary'. How would it be if you imagined two secretaries sitting on a tank (as there is square on Sec)? Or, if you think this might not clarify whether the square was on Tan or on Sec, you can visualize a tank with a secretary sitting on the top of it with a duck (image for the number 2) on her head ($Sec^2$).

This means when you have to create an image yourself, you have to really think logically about what may confuse you or what may not confuse you and what you normally or naturally remember. On the basis of your understanding of yourself, you can carry on making your own customized video file for each formula. Initially, it may look little confusing or difficult or time-consuming. But once you have done some of the fifteen to twenty formulae you will master this technique and there will be no more confusion thereafter.

CHAPTER 8

---

# HOW TO CREATE AN EMERGENCY MENTAL TOOL BOX

IMAGINE A situation where you are going on a journey or picnic in your favourite car along with your family and friends. Suddenly the car breaks down during the journey. In the absence of any mechanic for the next few hundred kilometres you are fully dependent on your emergency tool box and your knowledge of how to use it—not only for the continuance of the journey, but also to safeguard yourself and the other passengers as the road is surrounded by a thick jungle and has wild animals. Although the possibility of your falling into such a trap is near negligible, as a responsible driver, you should understand the importance of an emergency tool kit.

Now imagine that you have just moved abroad and one day you wake up to find that you have been robbed of your all belongings. You immediately try to pick up the phone to call your guardian/brother/sister/other relative/friend who lives there for immediate help, but you realize that your mobile is also missing and you do not remember their telephone or mobile numbers. And if you decide to reach out to them physically you need to know their address which you had saved in your laptop and, of course, the laptop is also stolen. Unluckily, the only telephone number which you remember is that of your office, which is not responding. The next option is to ask for help from a local cop in an alien city. The first thing that the cops ask for is your passport, which you have lost as it was kept in the laptop bag. Then they ask for the passport number. You are embarrassed to realize that you never paid any attention to the passport number; in spite of the fact that you wrote down your passport number several times while filling the immigration forms.

To cut a long story short, too much dependence on gadgets for maintaining your vital information including your blood group, ATM password, email password, email password retrieving information, spouse's phone number, home landline number, online banking passwords, transaction passwords etc. can bring out so much inconvenience. It is similar to being trapped in a broken down car without a proper tool box or the basic knowledge of how to use the tool box.

The only authentic gadget to record all the vital information is your own super computer, i.e. your brain.

**How to create a mental emergency tool kit:**

**Step 1**: You must make a list of vital information which you may be using often but are dependent on your gadgets or machines or diary every time you need them.

Here's a sample list of such information.

1. Passport number
2. Passport expiry date: Imagine that you never paid attention to it and a day before your next trip, you discover that your passport has expired.
3. Driving licence number: Imagine a situation where you have misplaced your driving licence and have not bothered to keep a photocopy.
4. Security information: Which you set for your online net banking transactions or during creating an email id. Now imagine a situation where you cannot recall the answers to the security questions or one where your email is hacked and you want to retrieve the password

and block the hacker but you don't even remember the basic information to do so.

5. Laptop passwords
6. Your locker number

And many more such vital information.

**Step 2**: Now you must keep such information in a place where you have 24x7 access but at the same time, it is out-of-bounds to others. This gadget, which can never be stolen or accessed by others, is your own super computer—your brain.

To store your personal information in your brain, I would suggest you create a 'memory journey' as per your own requirements. Your old school building may be perfect for this. Go back to your childhood memories and create a mental journey. For instance, take a look at the sample of my school journey:

1. School gate
2. Guard room
3. Administrative block
4. Cycle parking
5. Main building entrance
6. Principal's office
7. Teacher's room
8. Library
9. Playground
10. Canteen
11. Stairs
12. Water cooler
13. Classrooms

14. Chemistry lab
15. Physics lab

## Step 3

Now, decide to place each of the vital pieces of information collected in Step 1 on each stop of the school journey (refer to the Journey Method chapter). Further, to make it more usable and practical you may group the related information (like information regarding your bank account number, user name, login password, transaction password and ATM PIN) and put each of the groups in one part of your mental school journey, for instance, all bank-related information in the school library section.

Next, associate your bank account number with the librarian, your online transaction password with the library guard, and your ATM PIN with your favourite place to sit in the library.

## Step 4

To attach the information with the respective stops of the journey you have to rely for the most part on two methods. For all kinds of words—including passwords for emails, security question answers, etc.—you may use the Word Image System (WIS) and for numbers you may depend on the Number Method. Refer to the earlier chapters to do so.

## Step 5

The most important of all these steps is that you have to commit to yourself that whenever you have to refer to any of the information (which you have collected in Step 1) for day-to-day needs, rather than referring to conventional sources you must refer to this mental journey. This will not only help you in refreshing the journey but also strengthen the retention of information.

## How to create your personal emergency tool kit:

Now it's time to create your own emergency tool kit.

**Step 1**: To start with, think of the top five most important pieces of information which you would definitely like to put in your emergency mental tool box. Here is a suggested list.

1. ATM PIN
2. Local medical emergency number
3. Neighbour's phone number
4. Childcare number
5. Spouse's phone number

**Step 2:** Create your own journey from the memory of your school or any other source you like.

**Step 3:** Decide, how you would like to place the vital information in the journey stops. You may decide to group them or place them according to the convenience of the associations with the particular stops. To practice and gain a greater understanding of the techniques, write the clue to the respective information in the following blanks.

Associations for—

**Stop 1**.............................................

**Stop 2**.............................................

**Stop 3**.............................................

**Stop 4**.............................................

**Stop 5**.............................................

### How to create a mental first aid box:

Nobody can deny or underestimate the importance of remembering lifesaving medical tips in an emergency. Imagine that you are travelling on a train and a passenger near you becomes unconscious; your understanding of the medical emergency situations, ability to diagnose him correctly and carrying out timely first aid can play an important role in saving the ill person from damaging his organs further or may even save his life.

Here, your efficient and timely recollection of the lifesaving medical tips can play an important role.

Let's start with some common medical emergency situations.

## Situation 1

Children are standing in a queue at a school assembly and all of a sudden one faints and falls on the ground.

## Medical tips

1. Position the person on his or her back.
2. Check the person's airway to make sure it's clear. Watch for vomiting.
3. Check for signs of circulation (breathing, coughing or movement).
4. Give him fresh coconut water/fresh sweet lime juice (unless he is a diabetic) every half-hour for the next two hours.

### How to memorize the above steps

### Clue 1

Go back to your past memory of your entire school life and try to identify a similar situation of fainting, especially if it was someone you knew. That person can serve as a 'memory anchor' for learning the medical tip for fainting.

### Clue 2

Once you identify the person, imagine that you are giving him first aid in accordance with the first four medical tips.

Make sure that you are visualizing each and every step vividly. Now this is going to become the perfect and permanent video file and will help to recall the medical tips for fainting in case of future needs.

## The major memory rule

It really is very simple. For instance, think of 'cough and cold' and go back to the recent past. Think of a celebrity with whom you are able to associate or sympathise with: if you are among one of those who takes interest in political dramas you may promptly be able to connect the symptoms of cold and cough with, say, Arvind Kejriwal. This means to remember the medical tips for cough and cold your memory anchor will be Arvind Kejriwal. You just have to visualize that Kejriwal is following the suggested (see below) medical tips to cure himself of the ailment.

Now try to find your own memory anchors to memorize medical tips for the required medical situations. (Please remember that the list provided below is meant to act **only** as a memory-building exercise, and should **not** be taken as a substitute for medical advice from certified medical practitioners.)

| Medical Condition | Things to be done | To eat/drink |
|---|---|---|
| Stomach ache | Stop consuming anything solid for the next twelve hours. | Drink herbal tea twice an hour followed by fruit juice every two hours. |
| Diarrhoea/ Vomiting | Stop eating and take rest. | Consume coconut water every hour for next twelve hours and drink at least five to seven glasses of lemon water and honey. |

| Headache/ body ache | Stop consuming dairy products and grains for the next few hours. Massage the affected part with fresh aloe vera gel. | Drink herbal tea two to three times and coconut water (250 ml) after every two hours. |
|---|---|---|
| Fever | Take rest and put a cloth soaked in cold water on the chest and forehead for a few minutes. Repeat after every two hours till fever goes down. | Consume fruits and vegetable juice (three times a day) alternatively every hour for a day. |
| Cold/ Cough | Stop consuming fried, oily food and dairy products. Sip warm water every now and then. | Drink herbal tea, citrus fruit juice (four times a day) and consume mostly raw vegetables for at least three days. |

The usage of the **Memory Anchor Method** may not only be used in some common first aid but can also be extended to more complicated and serious illnesses.

For example, let us assume you want to memorize the symptoms, causes and treatment of tuberculosis as given below. Please remember that this list is meant to act only as a memory-building exercise and should not be taken as a substitute for medical advice from certified medical practitioners.

| TUBERCULOSIS | |
| --- | --- |
| **Causes** | **Symptoms** |
| • All cases of TB are passed from person to person via droplets.<br>• Crowded living conditions.<br>• Alcoholism.<br>• Improper lifestyle. | • Suffers from constant cough,<br>• Chronic fever in which temperature is higher in the evenings.<br>• Lack of appetite.<br>• Pain in the chest.<br>• Problem in breathing.<br>• Excessive mucus of yellowish color. |

**Cure:**
• Tuberculosis may also be treated with Indian gooseberry (Amla). Mix gooseberry juice with honey and take on a daily basis.
• Consume bottle gourd (lauki) juice, as it is one of the best vegetables for treating tuberculosis.

**Memory steps**

**Step 1**
Select your memory anchor and here you may deviate a little from the standard procedure of choosing a memory anchor. Say this time you may decide to choose your favourite film villain Ghajini from the movie *Ghajini*. Imagine Ghajini with all the symptoms in an exaggerated form.

For instance, imagine Ghajini's lungs hanging outside the body, his ears releasing smoke (chronic fever), his nose full of mucus running endlessly (constant cough). He is holding his chest with pain and is unable to eat.

**Step 2:**

Initially, you can create a complete video file of Ghajini involving the symptoms, dose and the treatment procedure. Here, your ability to exaggerate and make things amusing and larger than life will create an important role in creating a long lasting video file. For instance, imagine that Ghajini is sitting on a heap of gooseberries while drinking the juice through a lung pipe (similar to the one used by the fire brigade personnel).

You may now select some family members or friends from your circle to memorize the cure for most common medical conditions. Please note, once again, that the medical cures given in the above examples are only to illustrate the application of memory techniques, and not meant to be used without medical supervision.

-------------------------------------------------------------------

# CHAPTER 9

# APPLYING MEMORY TECHNIQUES
# TO BUSINESS STUDIES

THIS CHAPTER will help you to store and access large amounts of logical information. It is not only about memorising but also about understanding the concept. The idea is all about how to memorize information, vital in business studies, while understanding the concept. To understand the method let's look at an example.

**Question 1: What are the essential elements of a valid contract?**

**Answer:**

1. Agreement
2. Free consent
3. Competence of the parties
   (a) Major

(b) Sound mind

(c) Person not disqualified by law from contracting

4. Lawful consideration
5. Lawful object
6. Not expressly declared void
7. Intention to create legal relationship

**Answer:** One way of memorising this is by repeatedly reading it again and again i.e. by rote memorisation. Another method could be by understanding each and every point and then memorising it.

However, both of the above mentioned methods have three major drawbacks:

1. It takes more time to learn/memorize
2. The chances of forgetting/missing any point is high
3. More time is spent in recollection

Here, you may use a new method; I call it the **Imaginary Situation Method**. It will help you to not only understand the topic logically but also help you to convert the topic into a video file.

## The Imaginary Situation Method

**Step 1**: Think of an imaginary situation. For example, one day your father comes to talk to you and the conversation goes something like this, 'You are now grown up and I think it's time you got married,' and he sits with you for a long time to discuss your plans.

You don't want to get married at this time, and try to convince him that you need more time to take such a major decision. But he finally overcomes all your arguments and you give in to his wishes.

**Step 2:** Now keep this imaginary situation in mind and associate it with the topic you are studying (the question 'What are the essential elements of a valid contract?' and the answer), and you will be automatically able to create a video file on the topic.

Now let's go point by point as listed in the answer to Question 1 above.

1. Agreement: This is the first point you have to remember. So link it to the fact that the girl's preferences in terms of career, family etc. must match yours, which means an agreement on such important issues.
2. Free consent: This is the second point you have to remember. So link it to the fact that the girl should give free consent to the marriage.
3. Competence of the parties: She must be competent to marry i.e.
   (a) She must have attained the age of majority.
   (b) Must be of sound mind.
   (c) Should not have been disqualified by law.
4. Lawful consideration: You must keep lawful consideration in mind and not ask for unlawful things like dowry.
5. Lawful object: People should bring lawful objects like flowers or gifts into the marriage hall. No one should bring any unlawful objects such as revolvers, daggers, swords, hand grenades etc., to the marriage hall.

6. Not expressly declared void: To ensure that the marriage is not expressly declared void by law make sure that the girl is not already married as per Hindu law!

7. Intention to create legal relationship: Imagine that after the marriage ceremony the marriage hall suddenly changes into a court where a judge gives you a legal certificate of marriage and agrees that it is your intention to create a legal relationship.

To understand the Imaginary Situation Method, let's take one more example.

## Question 2: Legal rules regarding offer.

## Answer:

1. Offer must be capable of creating a legal relationship.
2. Offer must be certain, definite and not vague.
3. Offer may be expressed or implied.
4. Offer must be distinguished from an invitation to offer.
5. Offer may be specific or general.
6. Offer must be communicated to the person to whom it is made.
7. Offer must be made with a view to obtain consent of the offeree.
8. Offer may be conditional.
9. Offer should not contain a term, the non-compliance of which amounts to acceptance.
10. Communication of special terms.

Let's create a story using the Chain Method with the example cited for Question 1.

Now the scene to imagine is that your father is not

able to satisfy all the conditions specified by you, and so you need to search for a girl to marry on your own. Now what will you do?

1. First you need to propose to the girl by making her an offer/proposal to become your life partner/wife; in other words the offer must be capable of creating a legal relationship.

2. You must make her a certain and definite offer by asking her if she will marry you, rather than simply stating that you want to get married. A simple statement that you want to get married will not specify whether you want to marry her or someone else. In other words the offer must be certain, definite and not vague.

3. Your offer to marry her may also be expressed by your conduct. You show her the ring you have bought and put it on her finger; in other words the offer may be expressed or implied.

4. You must make an offer of marriage by telling her how well you can take care of her etc.; you must not invite her to marry by telling her how great you are. In other words the offer must be distinguished from an invitation to offer.

5. Your offer can be specific or general i.e., you can specifically make an offer of marriage, or you can place a classified matrimonial ad in a newspaper (general).

6. You must clearly communicate your offer to her, in other words the offer must be communicated to the person to whom it is made.

7. The offer must be made with a view to obtain her

consent. In other words the offer must be made with a view to obtain consent of the offeree.

8. You may impose some conditions like I will be able to marry you only after I complete my CA degree. In other words the offer may be conditional.

9. While making the offer, you can not say to her that if the offer is not accepted before a certain date, it will be presumed to have been accepted. In other words offer should not contain a term, the non-compliance of which amounts to acceptance.

10. You should communicate all special terms such as your likes/dislikes/preferences etc.

## How to select an imaginary situation for the Imaginary Situation Method:

There are three major resources from which you can cull an almost limitless number of imaginary situations.

**Source 1**: An experience or situation from your own life.

**Source 2**: An experience or situation from the life of someone near and dear to you.

**Source 3**: You may select a situation from any of your favourite movies.

Now consider the example below.

## Question 3: Define the roles of a commercial bank.

## Answer:

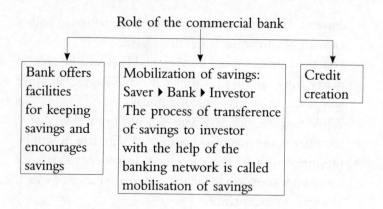

Role of the commercial bank

| Bank offers facilities for keeping savings and encourages savings | Mobilization of savings: Saver ▸ Bank ▸ Investor The process of transference of savings to investor with the help of the banking network is called mobilisation of savings | Credit creation |

## Functions of the bank

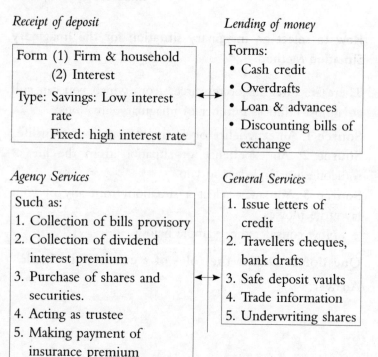

*Receipt of deposit*

Form (1) Firm & household
     (2) Interest
Type: Savings: Low interest rate
     Fixed: high interest rate

*Lending of money*

Forms:
• Cash credit
• Overdrafts
• Loan & advances
• Discounting bills of exchange

*Agency Services*

Such as:
1. Collection of bills provisory
2. Collection of dividend interest premium
3. Purchase of shares and securities.
4. Acting as trustee
5. Making payment of insurance premium

*General Services*

1. Issue letters of credit
2. Travellers cheques, bank drafts
3. Safe deposit vaults
4. Trade information
5. Underwriting shares

To select a situation which may help you memorize the above topic, think of a movie where bank-related scenes were shown prominently. I can instantly think of the movie *Baghban* where the hero Raj Malhotra (Amitabh Bachchan, whom we shall refer to as AB) works in a bank. Now you can easily superimpose this situation with the above topic you want to memorize. Remember, this example will be relevant to you only if you have seen this movie.

Have a look at how you can associate this situation with the topic.

1.  Mobilisation of savings: Bank manager AB is motivating people to open savings accounts in his bank. And he is giving savings bank account money for business investment to some investors, thus mobilising funds.

2.  Receipt of deposit: Bank manager AB gets the money from firms and households and he also charges interest for the money he gives to other investors.

3.  Lending of money: Bank manager AB gives whatever money he gets as loans and advances to his friends in need (can be a close friend) and he gives a discount to those who pay their bills before time (discounting bills of exchange).

4.  Agency Services: Bank manager AB is a very good and efficient person and he manages many other activities such as collecting dividend interest, making policy premiums and acting as trustee. His duties also include dealing in the share market.

5.  General Services: Bank Manager AB is also famous for

issuing travellers cheques, bank drafts, etc. Along with it he also issues Letters of Credit.

At this point it would be important to understand the factors which you should keep in mind to make the method effective and you must also learn to modify the method so as to fit your memory needs.

## Involve other senses to memorize better

Till now we have been focusing on the most important aspect of the brain, i.e. the video file. To make your memory work even more effectively you may involve other senses too.

Your brain can retain information even for a lifetime, while experiencing or learning the information, if the following senses are also involved directly or indirectly.

1. Hearing.
2. Seeing or visualising.
3. Touch.
4. Emotion and feeling (extreme positive or extreme negative).
5. Ability to associate or connect with the information.

There are three major memory senses which lead to learning.

1. Eye memory: learning through seeing or visualising in colour.
2. Ear memory: learning through listening.
3. Motor memory: learning through touch or body movement, while experiencing the information to be learnt.

## Formula for permanent learning

While experiencing information you must involve all the senses and dynamics of the brain for permanent learning.

**Ear memory + Eye memory + Motor memory + Emotion + Ability to associate with yourself (Self Association) = Long-term memory.**

We use more of the 'Ear memory' to memorize or understand an answer/a topic generally when we prepare for exams. Most students learn by reading the topic aloud or silently several times. In this method, students focus on hearing the sound of words to memorize. This way the information is retained for the short-term. Hence most students tend to forget it after some time.

### Game for Developing A Permanent Memory

**Question 4: How does one involve all the senses and the principle of the brain in memorising theory for permanent retention?**

**Answer 4**: While memorising a topic, play the game of 'Circle of FAMES', keeping in mind the rules of the game; it will automatically ensure the involvement of Eye memory + Ear memory + Motor memory +Self Association.

To remember the rules of the game you may call it the principle of FAMES.

F- Feeling and emotion
A- Association
M- Motor memory
E- Eye memory
S- Sound (Ear memory)

## How to play 'Circle of FAMES'

### Step 1:

Imagine that you are going to start a venture or a business
of your own
Decide the name of your venture/business:...............
Decide the product:.............

### Step 2:
### Appointments

To run a business you have to appoint some people.

1. Director
2. CEO
3. Partner
4. Accountant
5. Stockist
6. Distributor
7. ............
8. ...........
etc.

**Important:** While making such appointments you must
keep in mind the following rules.

1.  These people should be closely known to you. They can

be members of your family, from your circle of friends or a close acquaintance.

2. The selection should not be random. Heart + Brain = Appointment.

3. Assign each person a designation, for example:
   - Shareholder:.............
   - Partner:...........
   - Accountant:...........
   - Commissioner Vendor:.............
   - Vender/Supplier:...........
   - Distributor, etc.:............

The most important rule in the game is your ability to identify, select and appoint the right person for the right profile/designation.

**Rule: Deal with people**

In this method we have to reduce every activity or department into people.

One important aspect would be to connect the imagination with emotions, while imagining the situation with the people whom you have assigned a particular designation. Try to identify the emotion at the moment if any (love, hatred, concern, fear, anger, respect). Remember emotions are like glue for memory, **anything which you are able to feel, you are able to retain**.

We must 'appoint' only near and dear ones so that we are able to connect with them emotionally while visualizing them in the process of memorising. We know that emotion and feeling plays an important role in the process of retention. Imagining that you have appointed a stranger, or thinking of a particular designation or activity symbolically, will not help in long-term retention. Further, appointing near and dear ones will enhance your understanding of the subject. Scientifically, this is called 'neural-rewiring'. When you **mentally visualize** certain information, the brain registers the information better. In the world of sports, it is called 'latent learning'. All top athletes around the world use this science extensively to enhance their performance.

For instance, suppose you have to study a topic in Macro Economics, your 'appointments' may include the following.

1. Industrialist
2. Farmer
3. Executive
4. Tax Commissioner
5. People in different professions
6. Sometimes even Ministers to represent different sectors, etc.

## Question 5: How to choose the designation and appointment for a particular chapter/topic/subject?

**Answer 5:** Your ability to use this method will depend in a major way on your ability to choose the right designation and make the right appointment. For choosing the right designation/s for a particular topic, your understanding and knowledge of the given topic will be of great help.

**Important**: If you have 'appointed' a particular person say as a 'Tax Commissioner', then throughout your life whenever you study any topic where a Tax Commissioner finds a mention, you must refer to the mental picture of the same person. You must not change the character of this appointed person for any other subject or topic.

We may understand how to apply the Circle of Fames with the help of the following example.

**Question 6: Describe rights and duties of a partner.**

**Answer:**

## Rights of Partners

1. Right to take part in conduct of the business.
2. Right to be consulted.
3. Right to have access to, inspect and copy books of the firm.
4. Right to share profits equally if there is no agreement otherwise.
5. Interest on capital: Not allowed, but if otherwise partnership agreement provides for the payment of interest on capital, it shall be payable only out of profits.
6. Interest on advances given by the partner to the firm will be paid at the rate agreed, if there is no agreement to this effect, interest is allowed at the rate of six per cent per annum.
7. Right to be indemnified by the firm in respect of all expenses and liabilities incurred by him in the ordinary and proper conduct of business.
8. Right to remuneration: No remuneration allowed except if there is an expense agreement.
9. Right to stop admission of a new partner.
10. Right to retire with the consent of all other partners, where partnership is at will, by giving notice to that effect to all other partners.

11. Right not to be expelled from the firm by any majority of the partners.
12. Right of outgoing partner to share subsequent profits- the retiring partner of legal representatives of deceased partners has option—to share of profit or to interest at 6 per cent per annum on the amount of his share in property of the firm.
13. Right to dissolve the firm: with the consent of all partners, where partnership is at will the firm, may be dissolved by any partner(s) giving notice in writing to all other partners of his intention to dissolve the firm.
14. Right in emergency: a partner has the right to bind the firm for acts done in emergency, as are reasonably necessary for protecting the firm from loss; provided he has acted in the same manner as a man of ordinary prudence would have acted in like circumstances.

## Duties of Partners

1. Duty to carry on the business of the firm to the greatest common advantage.
2. Duty to account for profits earned:
   a) from any transaction of the firm; or
   b) from the use of firm's property; or
   c) business connection of the firm; or
   d) firm's name.
3. Duty not to carry on competing business to that of partnership firm:
   a) if it carries on it must be accounted for; and
   b) the firm will not be liable for any loss.

4. Duty to be just and faithful to each other.
5. Duty to render true accounts and full information, of all things affecting the firm, to any partner or his legal representatives.
6. Duty to indemnify the firm for any damage caused to it by reason of his fraud in conduct of firm's business.
7. Duty to attend diligently to his duties relating to conduct of firm's business.
8. Duty not to claim remuneration: Remuneration may be allowed to working partner provided there is specific agreement to that effect.
9. Duty to contribute equally to the loss sustained by the firm, unless otherwise agreed.
10. Duty to indemnity the firm for any loss caused to it by wilful neglect in the conduct of business of the firm.
11. Acquire immovable property on behalf of firm.
12. Transfer immovable property belonging to the firm.
13. Opening a bank account on behalf of the firm in his own name.
14. Enter into partnership on behalf of the firm.

In order to memorize the above mentioned rights and duties of a partner, first you need to identify your partner. Imagine that you want to set up your own business, now think of a person who best suits you as your business partner keeping in mind all the rules mentioned for 'Circle of Fames' above.

Now visualize the designated person as your partner in your mind; you need to identify your initial emotions and their intensity when you think of him/her.

Now associate all the rights and duties of a partner with

'your' partner and see him performing all assigned things in action, all pictures in colour. Involve all senses and emotions to learn it better.

Now keep a track of how your emotions change towards the partner when you see him/her performing all the duties and exercising all the rights. Note all the changes in your emotions and develop a good long-term memory.

# CHAPTER 10

---

# VIDEO FILES FOR ACHIEVING ANY GOAL IN LIFE

IN ALL these chapters, you have seen how video files can play an important role in memorising, retaining and recollecting information. But you will be amazed to see that the role of video files is not limited to learning alone. It plays an important role in the fulfilment of all kind of roles in life including career goals and health goals.

To understand the role of video files in the accomplishment of a goal, let's take the example of Major James Nesmith, an American soldier who was held captive during the North Vietnam war for seven years. He was confined to a very small cell where there was only a single source of sunlight in the form of a small hole in the roof.

During his entire time there, he was not allowed to speak to anyone, or meet anyone. Major Nesmith realized that the solitude would drive him crazy unless he had some way of inculcating positive thought into his daily routine.

That's when he learned to visualize. He had always dreamt of improving his golf but never had a chance to do so. What he now did was to visualize his favourite golf course and each day, he imagined playing a full eighteen holes at an imaginary country club. He pictured everything in great detail—the green of the course, the sun on his skin, the wind rustling the leaves of the trees around him and the smell of his sweat as he swung his clubs over and over across the course. He instructed himself to swing better, and followed his ball as it swung in an arc, and fell on the exact spot where he had wished it. And over time, the golf course became very real to him.

It took him a long, long time to play eighteen holes, since his detailing was so intricate. And when he was finally released, he played an actual tournament and won![1]

---

[1] A version of this popular urban legend also appears in *A Second Helping of Chicken Soup for the Soul* (HCI: 1996).

To understand how your imagination and video files play an important role in the accomplishment of any goal or task let's take a simple situation. Think of a situation where an extremely tired and fatigued boy is relaxing. He is so tired he feels he can't even stand. Suddenly he sees a barking dog biting a few people nearby and running towards him. So what do you think will be his next move?

1. He will sprint like a hare to save himself.
2. He will stay seated as he is too tired to move.

Actually his instant reaction would be to run even faster than his normal speed of running, in spite of the fact that he was too exhausted to even stand a minute ago. Let us pause to understand something about how the brain works.

Here, it is clear that whatever you practise—either physically, like practising running laps around the playground or mentally, as did Major James Nesmith—ultimately the video file of the practice is stored in the memory bank, and that is why it is said that 'practice makes perfect'.

All sportspersons over the world know this and religiously practise the way Major James Nesmith did. Once, after achieving a world record of thirty-five centuries, Sachin Tendulkar was asked the secret of success in cricket in an interview. He said, 'Before every match, I visualize in my mind that I will get a hundred. I did so before this match too. As pre-match preparation, I do certain things, this is one of those things.'

Mohammed Ali, the greatest boxer of the last century, in his biography, was unwittingly describing video files when he said, 'The man who has no imagination has no wings.' He used to visualize the expected win against his opponent for hours. He used to see each and every detail of it vividly.

You can call this method of achieving a goal the **Mental Rehearsal System (MRS)**. Once you understand the MRS, you will realize that in the past whenever you were successful, you unknowingly applied MRS.

The only thing which differentiates highly successful people from the rest, is that highly successful people use MRS more often.

## Mental Rehearsal System

MRS can be divided into four easy steps.

**Step 1:** The most important thing about achieving a goal is that you should be clear about what you want. You will agree with me that many of us remain undecided about our goal in life and it keeps fluctuating too often depending upon many factors including circumstances, the people around us, the inability to achieve success in our first attempt, criticism from others, etc.

If you do not know where you want to reach, you will not be any closer to your destination, no matter how good a driver you are.

**Step 2:** Once you have decided upon your goal, create a mental video of it. You should be able to see the video of a future where your goal has been accomplished. Remember that your brain does not distinguish between experiences that are real and events that have happened only in your mind. In neurological terms, when you imagine a vivid experience, your brain views it as real as your hand or the chair that you are sitting in. Nevertheless, the degree of success you achieve depends on two factors: repetition and emotion.

## Repetition

The most important feature about any habit is that you create it by repeating the same sequence or process again and again and again—not by doing it just once. This is how we learn several life-skills, including working, or talking, or even just holding a pen. This is true even for your imaginary goal.

Once most people have set a goal they treat it like a New Year resolution and never visit the idea again. And this is the major reason why people fail. You must make a provision where you get enough opportunity to visualize it again and again, every day, day after day for months or better still, till you achieve your goal.

## Emotion

Once you repeat a goal mentally to trigger the neurological pathway which converts your mental goal into an equivalent physical action, you have to **feel** the goal. The **excitement and the emotional connect** with the goal will not only play an important role in your attaining success, but also in improving your personality.

Once you start visualizing the goal several times a day, you will soon be able to **feel** as if you have already accomplished the goal. You will see a change in your behaviour—may be in your choices of food; you may find many new things interesting; maybe you will find some new friends, or may lose interest in some friend who is not connected or a bit distracted about your goal. Your brain will create bit by bit the personality which suits your imagined goal. This transformation may not happen overnight but you may see it happening with you once you take the first two steps.

**Step 1:** Creating an affirmation

An important thing in achieving a goal is by talking about it many times a day. Here your choice of words will play an important role. For example-

If you want to be thin and lean. There are two ways to say it:

1. I don't want to be fat.
2. I want to be slim.

Remember although both the sentences mean the same but your brain is not much influenced with the words like, 'I want 'or 'I don't want'. It is triggered by the words like 'fat' or 'thin'. The moment brain will hear fat it will connect the neural pathways to all the past memory of fat and that will lead to unwanted outcome to struggle the weight. Here, your choice of words will play an important role, so try to choose positive words which will connect you to the desired outcome.

**Step 2:** Prepare your own mental goal material.

Prepare material which will help to remind you of your goal several times a day. It may be in the form of:

1. A vision board
2. Written material
3. An audio recorded message
4. Any symbol, etc.

It is not important how much time you decide to devote to it, what is important is to do it. Now, try to visit the material every day, several times a day preferably at the same time. This is the key to successful mental conditioning.

All kinds of successful people including musicians, athletes or leaders do it. Routine practice four times a day for a few days at the same time and in the same place will have far more impact.

Find a place where you will not be disturbed for at least ten minutes. Turn off your mobile, and e-mail alerts which may interrupt you.

## Step 3

Feel the doubt and do it anyway. As you first go through this new daily process you may feel a nagging sense of discomfort or disagreement or a doubt. You may hear another voice in your head, 'No! It is not possible, you cannot be  this'; or 'You cannot do that'. Do not let this stop you, it is absolutely normal, it is the brain's warning response that you are entering a new territory. It is the brain's psycho-cybernetics response reminding you of your current state. The key is to feel it, sense it and appreciate the fact that the brain's psycho-cybernetic system is on work. So do not interpret it as a signal of not proceeding ahead in the direction of your chosen goal; let the sense of anxiety and discomfort translate into the thrill of adventure.

Now to understand it further let us consider the example of highly successful people and learn how they applied the above knowledge to leverage their success.

On 9 January 1970 Bruce Lee wrote a letter to himself titled: 'A secret letter to me'. In that letter he detailed his wishes for the next ten years, and wrote that till 1980 he would remain the most popular and successful actor. He always kept that letter in his pocket. The movie *Enter the Dragon* was released in 1973 and pushed him into the category of well-paid actors. Hollywood still treasures this letter. Is it not possible for us also to inculcate this kind of confidence to realize our dreams?

One of the writers of the bestselling *Chicken Soup for the Soul* series was asked the secret behind his success. He said that when he went to meet the publisher with his manuscript, he sent in his visiting card with the words, 'By 30th of January, 1994, more than 15 million copies of my books would be sold and I would be happy at my achievement.'

Often he used to look at this card. He believed that it was this confidence that led to his success; incidentally more than 80 million copies of his books have been sold in nearly thirty languages.

Now the question that arises is: What is the scientific connection between writing your dream in black and white and reading it again and again? Gandhiji said, 'If I believe that I can do something, I will do it, even though I may not have the potential in the beginning.'

It is written in the Bhagavad Gita that faith/confidence is the real test of a person. The holy Bible says, 'As a man thinketh in his heart so is he.'

It has been established beyond any doubt that those who live by their dreams actually do realize them. In fact this belief has a scientific basis to it. There is always a definite connection between what you believe and your aims.

Until 1954, it was believed that the human body is made in such a way that despite any runner's best intentions he/she could not cover the distance of a mile in less than four minutes. Then in 1954, Roger Bannister covered the same distance in three minutes and 59 seconds. What is even more surprising is that by the end of that year, thirty-two other people had achieved the same feat. In the next three years, about 200 people in the world covered the distance in less than four minutes. How come something that had been considered impossible for thousands of years became possible, suddenly?

The others got their inspiration from Roger but from where did Roger get his? When he was asked this question he replied that he had imagined himself achieving this feat. Imagining repeatedly what you want to achieve is called 'latent learning'. Most of the sportsmen of the world have transformed their dreams into reality on the basis of their imagination.

This does not mean that you should indulge in wild, meaningless imagination. If you imagine that you won't get hurt even after jumping from the fifth floor, you are being foolish. Latent learning does not mean that you should not use your mind at all. It means that we should imagine achieving our goal successfully, towards which we have been working so hard. If success is four steps away, then three steps have to be taken through sheer hard work and the fourth one through latent learning. If you work hard and ignore latent learning you can move only three steps. And if you indulge in pessimistic and negative latent learning you may even go a step backwards.

For example, when you reach the examination hall or the interview room, your heart starts thumping inside you and your throat gets dry. You almost lose control over yourself.

This is the result of negative latent learning. While preparing you were thinking that this exam would be very difficult. If you think that the lessons you have not learnt well are bound to feature in the question paper, then surely the same will come true.

This fact is related to the mutual contact of the mind and the body. There is some relation between the two and they meet in the state that we call imagination. When we think of a specific target, both our mind and body start preparing for it. When that moment arrives in reality, everything falls in place and things start happening according to our plans.

Often sportsmen have to come up to the expectations of millions of fans. If they get tense their targets move farther away from them. Remember what you imagine reflects in your actions and affects the body.

As an example, let us conduct an experiment. Close your eyes and imagine you have an orange in your right hand. You are peeling it with both hands. Now you are inhaling the flavour of the orange and as you bring it closer to your nose, the scent starts becoming stronger. Now imagine that you are squeezing the orange and that you can even feel the taste in your mouth.

Did you notice that as you imagined the orange your mouth started watering and you could even feel the taste? This goes to prove that there is a definite link between the mind and the body.

Our body works according to our thinking, you can easily walk on a wall that is one foot high and two feet wide but if the height is increased to a hundred feet, would you be able to walk on it?

Our actions are connected to our emotions and emotions are related to faith, belief and confidence. Positive thinking leads to positive emotions and you move aggressively towards the fulfilment of your desires.

'An idea can change your life'—you must have heard this line often on TV. It is very true. You do not really have to go anywhere for ideas, they are there in your mind. Einstein once said that imagination is more important than knowledge. Let us find out the scientific basis of the relation between imagination and ideas.

As an example, let us take the case of an island near Japan. The inhabitants of the island are monkeys, who live on the fruits and vegetables that grow on the island. Sweet potatoes also grow on the island but the monkeys never ate them because of the mud around the vegetables. Once while a monkey was playing with it, the sweet potato fell in water. Now it was nice and clean and the colour changed too. Out of curiosity the monkey tasted it and found it delicious. The other monkeys observed all this. After some time all of them started washing the sweet potato and eating it.

This is nothing great. Living beings learn from each other. But scientists were surprised when they learnt that thousands of miles away on another island, monkeys had begun behaving in a similar way, despite the fact that there was no connection between the two. The islands were situated at such a long distance from each other that swimming across from one to the other was impossible.

The scientists finally came to the conclusion that just as the radio catches signals from the atmosphere, so does the brain. All ideas, mind and wisdom are part of this universe as we are. Swami Vivekananda once said that when we tune the antenna of our mind i.e., when we think about a particular goal with full faith and without any trace of doubt, we get connected with the infinite wisdom of the universe; the chances of that 'desired idea' coming to our mind increases manifold. If you have thought of something new, always remember that other like-minded people can also think about it anytime.

You must have often heard that when some scientist talks about his invention, someone else from some other remote corner of the world also claims to have invented the same thing. Is this a case of plagiarism? No.

The fact is whenever one person hits upon an idea, the chances of someone else thinking about the same start increasing. If you have a problem or a question, definitely there is a solution and an answer to that somewhere in the universe. Bruce Lee wrote a letter to remind himself constantly about his goal. Einstein also admitted that he got his ideas from within himself.

Let us take the example of the invention of the sewing machine. The inventor made the needle but could not imagine how it would be possible to run a thread through it. Once he dreamt of some tribals coming towards him with spears in their hands. Each spear had an eye on the tip. The dream gave him an idea that a hole could be made at the tip of the needle. It goes without saying that whenever we look for an answer to a question in our mind, we must wait for a hint from the mind itself and the moment we get the hint we must apply it in our lives.

As a concluding example, I will mention my favourite motivational story of the Hungarian pistol champion Károly Takács. He was working with the Hungarian army and accidentally shot himself through the very right hand which had made him the pistol champion. The entire nation was in shock thinking that Károly Takács's career had ended and so had their hopes of their nation winning an Olympic medal.

But Károly had different plans. He secretly started practising with his left hand and it took him only six months to deliver similar results with the previously untrained left hand.

He won a number of championships, including the Olympic gold, with his left hand. The accident did destroy his right hand but not the video file of the skill which was still intact in his memory, and which helped him to transfer the same skill to his left hand within a short period of six months.

## CHAPTER 11

------------------------------------------------------------

# HOW TO THINK LIKE A MEMORY GENIUS

WELCOME TO the last chapter. We are towards the end of our journey, the journey towards a better memory. Through all these ten chapters you have understood that there is nothing called a good or bad memory; it is all about a trained or untrained memory; and there are certain tricks, certain methods and principles on the basis of which you can really work wonders. For instance, if you have a car, an excellent one, the only thing that you as a driver must follow are certain rules of driving and that will make the journey not only interesting and fun but also efficient. That would be a joy and that is what my aim is—that you should be an expert driver, able to steer your brain towards the results that you want.

Since childhood we have been trained in everything— how to hold a pen, how to walk, how to ride, how to hold a spoon or eat with a fork. Today we do all these things efficiently and effortlessly; we have done these things so many times that we have forgotten that there was a time when we did not know these things and we had to learn them. Now, we are doing all this without even being conscious about it.

Just remember the day when you started learning driving and you held the steering wheel for the first time; the very first day driving was scary and you were praying you would not ram somebody; every time you decided to press the brake you had to consciously see where the brakes were located and by the time you pushed the brake you were already about a hundred metres ahead of where you planned to stop. But then you saw hundreds and thousands of people driving efficiently and this meant it was possible. And, now at this moment, not only can you drive efficiently but you can also talk to your friend on the next seat, while simultaneously changing the CD in your music player.

All this happened only when you learned the method of driving and utilized that skill many times. I mean to say that all the techniques that you have learnt in this book—the Journey Method, the Association Method, the Shape Method or the Word Image System (WIS)—may initially appear a little different and unfamiliar, but once you have tried the techniques a few times, they will become second nature to you. It will become as automatic as your driving is today. Similarly, through practising these techniques well, not only will your brain become smarter but you will also be able to use two important memories that is 'ear memory' and 'motor memory', and by these I mean the kinesthetic ability of the body—your sense of feelings and emotion.

And this will happen only when you use these methods again and again. The major difficulty which I face when I train people on memory techniques is that initially students think that it may not be practical. Then I tell them that they have to practise repeatedly until it becomes second nature. Finally, only those who actually practise are able to see the results.

So many times in this world we see tasks and feel that we can tackle them easily. Can we? Let us do a small experiment to understand this better. Look at this box and take a minute and tell me how many times you can spot the alphabet 'f'.

# Believing  is seeing

# FINISHED FILES ARE THE RE-SULTS OF YEARS OF SCIENT-IFIC STUDY COMBINED WITH THE EXPERIENCE OF YEARS

How many did you spot? Write your answer here: ----------.

Okay! I know your answer might be 3, or, for some people, 4 or 7 or 5! But do you think all answers are correct? So before you count again, if you have some friends over ask them to count and record their answer. You will be surprised to see that everyone gives a different answer.

The correct answer is 6. Most of the time, people are wrong on their first attempt. With this example just try to understand how the brain works—the moment you looked at this picture, your brain tried to get a feedback from your subconscious memory as to how many times you expected to see 'f' in that sentence. You subconscious memory responds: 'maybe 3 or 4'. Now it is the job of the brain to prove your subconscious memory right, so it counts either 3 or 4 and hides the remaining 'f's from you; because one the jobs of the brain is to satisfy you. What I mean to say is that whatever you believe, your brain interprets the world as per your belief system.

So, if your belief can play such an important role, why not train your brain to believe that the world is a wonderful place where you can achieve all your goals? So here also I challenge and motivate you to take it further by believing that you can think like a 'memory genius'. If you decide to believe that when you use these techniques, you will be more efficient than ever, and you will find that you have mastered these techniques quite quickly—maybe in ten or fifteen days, if you devote a few hours each day towards it. The steps towards thinking like a memory genius are as follows:

**Step 1**: You have to take in the information correctly, so unless you know what you need to memorize, your brain cannot help you. This means once you **decide** what you have to learn, only then can you apply the techniques. It is so simple, but most of the time people don't pay attention to this.

Let us assume that in Step 1 you have taken a decision. Taking a decision is very important—unless you **decide to memorize**, how can you expect your brain to put in all the effort?

Here is an example of how the brain doesn't automatically remember even our own actions.

> You have a pen in your hand and are writing. Then your friend suddenly arrives and you begin talking to him. While talking, you automatically put your hand in your pocket and release the pen. Now your hand is in your pocket but it is no longer holding the pen. Then your friend says he has to go, and you take your hand out of the pocket to wave goodbye to him.
>
> Now you need the pen to finish what you were writing and you start looking for it here and there; when you do not find it you say, 'Oh God! Now where on earth did I put it?' and decide you have forgotten where you put it!

The fact of the matter is that you have not 'forgotten' because you never 'memorized' where you put it in the first place. You slipped your hand into your pocket while talking to your friend and automatically released the pen; an unconscious action of the brain; and your brain never recorded it. Since it is something that your brain has never recorded, how is it possible to retrieve that information?

Here's another example. Imagine the brain is like a

cupboard and remember you can only expect to retrieve that information from it, which you have placed in it. You cannot take out something you never **remember** placing in it, no matter how hard you try.

For your brain, the first and most important thing is the decision that 'I have to memorize this!'. And this will give you a clue why people sometimes become absentminded. Sometimes you go from one place to another to get something and by the time you reach there you find your mind is blank, because while you were moving you had some other issues which were displaying in your visual brain. This pushed your basic reason for moving from one place to another into some corner of the mind where it was hidden. That is how the brain works sometimes, we call it absent-mindedness.

You might have heard that Albert Einstein used to call his wife many times to ask her whether he had eaten lunch or not, because while eating he was mentally engaged with his experiments and lab. This means that he physically ate lunch but his brain never recorded that action. Something that the brain has never recorded becomes very difficult for it to recall later. The brain has its own method for doing things efficiently.

For example just imagine that you are crossing a busy road. You see various vehicles coming at ever changing speeds. By estimating the changing speeds of various cars, estimating the fixed distance of the road, and managing your variable speed you are successfully able to cross the road. The brain blocks all information it does not deem necessary such as any vehicle at a very far distance which may not be a hurdle in crossing the road.

The brain tries to record what you want to memorize so you must understand the importance of this—that the brain doesn't automatically learn; you have to tell the brain that there is something which you want to memorize. Then the brain decides to focus on it, and this means it will switch off some other peripheral things which may not be important at that moment.

**Step 2:** You have to ask yourself which category—audio file or video file—each item falls under. For me, this process is now automatic. Initially, I used to remind myself that before I learn I must ask whether it is of an audio or video nature. Once I knew it was of an audio nature it was clear that even if I memorized or revised it several times, I might not be able to retain it because of its audio nature. Audio category files are difficult to memorize as described in the previous 10 chapters, while a video file format can be retained for a long period by simply experiencing it or feeling it mentally.

In case it is an audio file, I go to Step 3.

**Step 3:** Convert that audio file to a video file. Before converting the audio file to a video file I must remind myself of the available methods which can help me to do that. So when you have to categorize audio files most of them can be categorized into two groups or at most three groups:

**Group 1:** Something numerical
**Group 2:** Words
**Group 3:** Diagram or an unknown shape

Now you know with the help of all those ten chapters, if it is a number then you have a method called the Number Method and also a method called the Shape Method, so you can promptly use it. For example, let's say below is a table you want to memorize:

| Organism | Chromosome number in each body cell | Memory Anchors |
|----------|-------------------------------------|----------------|
| Roundworm | 2 | Duck |
| Mosquito | 6 | Hockey Stick |
| Frog | 26 | NaG |
| Rat | 42 | RaiN |
| Human Being | 46 | RaJa |
| Guinea Pig | 64 | JaR |
| Gold Fish | 100 | TheSiS |
| Sunflower | 34 | MaRe |
| Garden Pea | 14 | TaRa |
| Maize | 20 | NaSa |
| Rice | 24 | NaRi |
| Onion | 16 | TaJ |

The first column contains a list that is easily recalled as a video file, so you don't have to worry about it. But chromosome numbers in the middle column (2 or 6 or 26), are of course audio files. Since you know these are numbers, you could use the Shape Method or the Number Method. I personally prefer the Shape Method for a single digit, and the Number Method for a double digit.

That means if I want to memorize details about the

roundworm my mental picture is a huge gigantic, round, worm. But '2' I know is the shape of a 'duck' as per the Shape Method so I can visualize a duck eating a round worm.

In the case of a frog I can see that the number of chromosomes are 26; this means I have to associate 26 with the frog, but 26 is an audio file. This being a double digit I can easily convert that number using the Number Method and the picture for 26 is NaG (n=2, g=6). So NaG and frog can be associated mentally—if I see a fight between NaG and frog. Now, as a video file, I know that I will be able to retain it for the long term.

Similarly, the onion has 16 chromosomes. Now 16 is an audio file but in the Number Method 1 is t or d and 6 is j or G so you can select like this—

1 = T

and

2 = j

Mental picture is 'Taj'

Your mental picture for 16 could be—Taj Mahal. You can imagine that the Taj Mahal is full of onions. I know it is ridiculous but that's what will help you to learn it faster. Similarly you can do it for the rest of the table. You will be able to do this only when you first understand that if the nature of the audio file is numbers then automatically you have to use the method made for numbers.

Consider another example.

## DEFECT OF VISION

Summary defect of vision and their correction

| Type of Defect | Effect of Defect | Correction |
|---|---|---|
| 1. Hypermetropia (Long sightedness) | Nearby objects not clearly visible | By using convex lens of suitable power |
| 2. Myopia (Short sightedness) | Distant objects are not clearly visible | By using concave lens of suitable power |
| 3. Astigmatism | Rays from one direction do not focus at one point | Cylindrical lenses |

Here in this table you can see the types of defects, effects and correction of vision. The first row talks of hypermetropia and the second of myopia. Here, if you somehow remember that myopia means a 'distant object not clearly visible', you will automatically remember the meaning of hypermetropia which is just the opposite of myopia. This means out of the two rows you have to only choose one row to memorize and logically you will understand the meaning of the other.

Suppose you choose the word myopia, you need to use WIS to convert it to a video file. I can imagine that 'my-piya' (in Hindi it means 'my darling') is coming from far away and I cannot recognise him correctly; is he my-piya or someone else's piya! So far so good, but we have to remember how to correct myopia too—with the use of concave lenses.

The word 'concave' is an audio file so we can quickly use WIS and convert concave into an image of 'cave'. Now my final mental picture could be that I am standing at one end of a very long cave and my piya is coming from the other end, but I am unable to recognise him because of the distance. If you visualize this one mental picture, it can help you to remember this complete table with all the information. So, this means once you are clear about what myopia is, you can know what hypermertopia is, because logically you know it is just the reverse of myopia.

Here you have understood what played an important role—some logic, common sense, science and a little bit of memory technique; and you become efficient.

Similarly, try to learn another table, the difference between fusion and fission.

## DEFERENCE BETWEEN FUSION AND FISSION

| Fusion | Fission |
|---|---|
| 1. In a fusion reaction, two light nuclei combine to from a heavy nucleus. | 1. In fission reaction, a heavy nucleus breaks up to form two lighter nuclei. |
| 2. It is not a chain reaction. | 2. It is a chain reaction. |
| 3. These reactions are uncontrolled. | 3. These reactions have been controlled to generate electricity. |
| 4. Energy produced in fusion reactions is more than produced during fission. | 4. Nuclear fission produces a large amount of energy. |
| 5. It occurs at very high temperature of the order of 107°C. | 5. It occurs at low temperature. |

**Step 1:** Focus on the heading: Fusion and fission.
**Step 2:** You have to ask whether it is an audio file or video

file. It is, of course, an audio file.

**Step 3**: Out of the two let's convert one rather than both in video file using WIS. Let's chose fission!......... fish. That means if you connect everything with fish in the second column it will help you to recollect or to remember the main features of fission. If you memorize the important features of fission you need not worry about fusion because logically, since you are a student of science, you do understand that fusion is normally the opposite of fission.

Now in fission the first point is that the heavy nucleus breaks up into two lighter nuclei. Here one becomes two— mentally picture a very big fish converting into two smaller fish; and those two smaller fish turning into four smaller fish and further forming into a chain of fish. You can easily memorize it as all the smaller fish together make a long chain and finally controlled to produce electrical energy. I could imagine them running some electrical gadgets and producing large amounts of energy sufficient for a town. Now, you are trying to check the temperature of fish and its falling very low. So this small mental video will not only help you to memorize fission it will also help you to memorize fusion as you know it is roughly the opposite of fission.

**Step 4**: Don't forget to revise the information.

1. When you sit for studies how about taking a ten- to fifteen-minute break after every fifty minutes of memorising? During that break whatever you have memorized through video files or through all these techniques your brain gets time to re-organize, re-store and re-plan that information.

Let's say there are two students and both have planned to study from 4:00 to 8:00 p.m.. One student studies continuously from 4:00 to 8:00 p.m., that is for a total of four hours, while the second studies from 4:00 to 8:00 p.m. with a ten-minute break every fifty minutes, roughly taking a total break of half-an-hour in all. This means that he has effectively studied for three-and-a half hours.

Interestingly, it is this second student who will be able to remember the matter for a longer period. That's how the brain works; this technique is called 'Spaced Learning'.

In each ten-minute break, this student moved around, listened to music or drank water. In this manner, he allowed his brain to re-capture, re-plan, and re-store and thus manage the learnt information.

The second most important thing in managing information for the long-term is revision.

## The simple technique of revision

Whatever you memorize now, you must revise within **24 hours**. In other words, your first revision should be in 24 hours. The second and the final revision should be in **a week's time**. If you ensure these two revisions, it will ensure long-term recall.

While revising it is imperative that you recall the same mental video file that you created while making the first attempt to memorize the information. This will help you to learn things lifelong.

Memorising is a mental sport. If you utilise this mental sport, you will not only be ahead of the rest but will also learn things faster and retain them long-term as well. It is like exercising your brain and this will keep your brain young. If your brain is young, it will be able to function better. Your brain has complete responsibility for all the metabolic chemical reactions happening in your body and the brain is able to perform them efficiently only when it is young.

Now, you are approaching the end of the book and it's time to test your brand new memory. Let's put ourselves in some real-life situations to understand how your memory works after understanding these techniques.

Imagine that you are at a meeting or a party and you are introduced to a new person. Let us say his name is Deepak.

At this moment, you have decided to use the memory technique which you have learnt from this book so that you remember his name. But immediately, the second thought that strikes you is that there is not a single example in this entire book on 'how to remember people and faces'. At this point, I must tell you that it is practically impossible to include every kind of situation that you may come across in your lifetime in the confines of a single book. So the first simple step, when you encounter some situation where you do not know how you can put your memory to best use, is to try to remember the Secret Memory Formula.

## Video File >Memory Leakage Hole >Audio File

This means that you have to convert whatever you want to memorize into a video file. Now focus on the name you want to remember, in this case, say, Deepak. It is a fairly common name and you probably already know somebody called Deepak. If yes, then your job is done—this means, the moment you come across a new Deepak you have to recall the old Deepak.

Then the second step is to associate that mental picture of the old Deepak with the new Deepak's face. How to do it? Note the face of the new Deepak very carefully. When you observe any new face closely, you may find something unusual depending on your observation skills. Initially, you may not be able to identify much in the first few faces but soon you will become proficient and skilful and find something to highlight or something unusual about the person's face.

For example, the new Deepak's nose could be a little longer than normal; this means you have to associate the nose of the new Deepak with the old Deepak by imagining him with this nose.

And then you may observe some special mannerism—maybe the way he laughs, maybe the way he stands; and you can link that mannerism with the old Deepak whom you are imagining.

While you are having a conversation with the new Deepak try to use his name frequently in your conversation. This way you have increased the chances of memorising his name and it will ensure that next time you meet him, his nose or body language will immediately remind you of the old and familiar Deepak and give you the clue that his name is also Deepak. Once you try this technique or method with a few names and faces, you will become more comfortable with it.

Now let us assume that you meet a new person and the name is totally unfamiliar. How you will remember him?

Here is how I did it. In 2012, at one of our 'International Record Breakers' Festival', we invited some international delegates to our place and one of them was Thuvan from Vietnam. Now this name is very unusual for most of us, this means it definitely is an audio file where there is no previous picture associated with this name.

Here, I was left with one technique, i.e. WIS. So the moment I heard that her name was Thuvan, automatically my mind could see a picture of a van. Now, for the next step I had to observe her face to find something unusual. She had a wide and generous smile—that was one thing; the second was that she was tall; and the third that her hair was a little curly. This meant I had to associate these things with Thuvan. I imagined a van that a girl was driving. Her smile was bigger than the dashboard of the van and her hair was flying in the air while she was driving the van.

In other words I had to associate the unusual things about the new face with something resembling the name, while observing the person carefully.

Now, let us consider another situation—you have decided to learn Italian. Now this means that you have to learn about 2000 new words in the Italian language. Simply remember the only thing which will help you to learn everything, which is the following formula.

## Video File >Memory Leakage Hole >Audio File

This means whatever you are going to learn or memorize, you simply need to convert into a video file. For example, let's say I give you a fictitious foreign word 'kavya' that means piglet. When I say piglet automatically you imagine a 'piglet' and when you say 'kavya' it is a new word. So you need to convert it to a video file using the WIS. You can start by thinking kavya…kavya…kavya means kavita or poem in Hindi. You can imagine that some piglets are writing a poem. They are acting like poets, so the next time when you come across some piglets you will see a little herd of poets. So next time in your foreign language class when your teacher asks you what kavya stands for you will automatically get a mental picture of piglets writing poetry: 'kavya'.

So I mean whether you talk of a foreign word or a new English word it doesn't make any difference to your brain and the only rule is that whatever the new word is, you just have to convert that into a video file using WIS.

Let me put you in one more interesting situation—say you have decided to set a world record for having the best memory and you go to a memory championship thinking that you know all these special techniques like the number system or WIS and you can really learn faster than the other people in the competition, plus you have also put in adequate practice. Now you are set for the World Memory Championship. There you are given a paper with this number series to memorize:

10 00 11 11 01 01 10 01 …..

That means you have to memorize fifty binary digits in less than four minutes. If you think logically you will realize that this series just consists of four different combinations—00, 01, 10 and 11. This means whatever be the length of the number series you must have video files to remember these four things. You have to only convert these four digits into four different video files. Through this book you have a corresponding file for each of these four symbols:

01: think of a 'stick' using the Shape Method

10: 'bat and ball' using the Shape Method

Similarly, 11 is dada (1=d, 1=d) through the Number Method, or for 11 you can use the Shape Method that is 'road' and the last is 00—my favourite—for which I can imagine two eyes.

So to remember this number series quickly, use the Journey Method. For this you have to keep on placing the pair of digits in a given sequence and that will help you to memorize even a fifty-digit binary number in less than five minutes.

Nevertheless, this achievement alone will not enable you to fulfil the criteria for world records or national records but you may be able to fulfil the criteria for 'Junior Grand Master' or 'Grandmaster'. In case you are interested you may contact the *India Book of Records* and they will guide you on how you can add one more feather to your other achievements. I wish you all the best and hope to meet you again, through some of my books and my memory workshops.

# ACKNOWLEDGEMENTS

I am especially thankful to my sister Rinki for her kindness and devotion, and for her endless support in taking care of my baby during my writing days; her selflessness will always be remembered.

I'm filled with gratitude for my mother Anjali Devi, who did all she could do for me. The odds were against her but she endured and defeated them. I'm obliged to my father, Satendra Kumar Tomar, who motivated me to be the best I could be. I'm thankful for my husband Biswaroop Roy Chowdhury who has stood by my side through the good, the bad, and the ugly.

I'm thankful for my daughter Ivy and my younger brother Anjul, both of whom I love unconditionally. There's nothing more important in the world than setting a good example for them.

I'm thankful to my friend and cartoonist Bijan Samaddar for the hard work he put in to finish the illustrations for this book on time. I thank Shankar Koranga, the graphic designer, for his help in formatting the book. Last, but not least, I am grateful to my friend Savita Rawat for her direction and for the generous chunk of time she spent on my book, which effectively helped me finish the project on time.